FLORIDA FOLK
HOMESTYLE POETRY

FLORIDA FOLK HOMESTYLE POETRY

SAM RAVEN

To order additional copies of this book, contact:
Xlibris
844-714-8691
www.Xlibris.com
Orders@Xlibris.com
823774

CONTENTS

FOREWORD

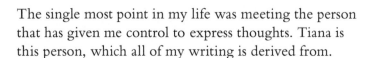

The single most point in my life was meeting the person
that has given me control to express thoughts. Tiana is
this person, which all of my writing is derived from.

Together in the military, my life was marked with her unbiased
kindness for other people, help given when problems arose!
Without her care, understanding, and intelligence, I would
certainly be dead; and without her encouragement, most
assuredly not invested in the production of this book.

I have multiple verses, three of which are about and to
Tiana. They are *"Tiana,"* *"My Friend,"* and *"Time."*

In regarding these verses, please let my thoughts be the
thoughts of humanity, so that everyone may understand.

When reading, please enjoy, for I feel most
everyone can try to relate, in a fashion.

SANDY

To allow me the true love and beauty of the
one siren I see constantly, in depths of my mind.
Out of the shadows she appears, black hair, dark eyes,
glistening skin.
Into the depths of my soul, she looks, always aware of the emptiness.
To love one, endless thought in mind, soul,
and body; alike but different.
Together but apart, always knowing,
struggling to reach the unseen apex of the ladder of life,
to achieve supremacy over the things that one dreads,
behold, the signs of earthly days, are they not the as eons past?
humanity continually tries to change.
The Earth, does not, in your game of life, how, will you cast your lot?
For the love that we once shared, time has increased a hidden love!
"From me to thee!"

YOU AND ME

I enjoy *new* things for me with *you*.
Everyday adventures are still alive.
Simple tasks are more important feeling as though
appreciation is exclaimed in every task or feeling.
Most *physical* acts are no longer manifest, just
placed in different order and areas of *need*!

SWEETEST STORY EVER TOLD

An unfilled longing for you, tender sound of
voice calms *wild* days and nights,
Feelings derived from being apart together in mind, spirit, soul.
What and When will final togetherness *be*?
Loving, sensing, ever-knowing, beautiful mind.
Gentle caress of your satin skin, ultimate
pleasure of feeling your gentle touch!
Just being close to *you* gives me a feeling *I*
have never experienced or felt before!
Calmness, peace, pleasure, *contentment*!

THE HOOT OWL

Owl is wide awake in the middle of the night. Their *big
wide eyes* are made for sight in the middle of the night!
Sounds they make isn't a whistle or toot, but a deep
signing that sounds like *Hoo-A-Hoot-Hoooo*.
Mice and rodents are not safe when Owl
is looking for a nightly snack.
Flying at night thru brush and trees is normal for this Bird of Prey.
Different types you may see are Barn Owl, Great Horned Owl,
Screech Owl, and the white with dark spots Snow Owl.
Young owls not quite grown yet are known as *owlets*, not to be
confused with the story of Pooh Bear, Tigger, and Little Owlet.

WINGS OF

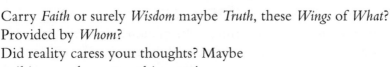

Carry *Faith* or surely *Wisdom* maybe *Truth*, these *Wings* of *What*?
Provided by *Whom*?
Did reality caress your thoughts? Maybe
striking nearby *not* touching *you*!
Then these *Wings* come into play, flying unseen
with energy imposed by unnatural hands.
Things happen that no one can predict or explain
benefiting all you, me, mankind!
Grasping parcels spread out on life's vast table envisions *flight of.*
Once said *To Fly With Wings of Eagles*, meaning your
thoughts determine your path through life, *easy or not.*
You must test your *wings so Wings of Faith* can come into play.
If strong, you will survive.
If *not*, you are earthly bound.
Wings of Life *do* abound and *can* raise you from being
down in this fall from grace *or* space of time.
Please remember to *fly* through.
This life requires a lot of unseen help with *two strong ... Wings of Faith!*

WIND

Flowing winds of wisdom carry *Wings of Faith* over ebb and
flow above and below, ever turning tides of humanity strife.
Hearing not the call, life trudges forth. Without
a cause, life is left to *waste* above this all.
In unseen fog, life's child wanders alone just him and his dog.
To say this is *nothing at all* shows how mankind has begun to fall.
Reality glows and a real person knows that *flowing* winds
tell that wisdom carries forth *Wings of Faith* to rise or fall
above or below ever-turning tides of *Human Daily Strife!*

WAR!

Castigating verbal prowess throwing away literate memories
enhancing world's population amidst streams of *pure* thought
while worldly ventures try selling stagnation of WAR!
Replacing fertile fields of producing edible foods, to
enlisting fertile minds to do battle, thus increasing revenue
and creating jobs by producing objects used in WAR!
Verbal conversations turn into commands resurrecting a
patriotic spirit giving cause and steadfastness towards a goal.
Attacking reasons, goals, and way of life/death is
not so bad *if* there is no hope for a better life.
Why cast shadows when there is no sun?
Help is but knowledge given free without issues
of claim. Surmise today of a sheep that lost its way
how you *search* to find; if you search to find,
In doing so *is it with LOVE*, not reprimand!

THE RANCH

Nestled deep in the secluded area of mind entering
thoughts that arise in periods of independence.
Days of hope breaking free from confinement
instilled through *necessity*!
Serene, quiet, natural being-one-with-nature,
not to destroy, but to let *nature* remain dominant.
Living in today's world to conserve, *never* forgetting
nature is a loving child of *Mother Earth*.

UNCLE HENRY & THE BOYS

Long days of summer filled with camping, fishing, and swimming
was had by all when Uncle Henry took his family for vacation.
When fall breezes begin to blow, dog pen activity starts to show.
Last year's hounds sense hunting time. Added are a
few young dogs to speed up the race for Henry &
the Boys in the Robinson hunting camp.
Lunchtime when all would gather someplace in the
woods to eat, practical joking took place.
When someone shot and killed a *buck* deer, riotous times
with guts flying wild was a mandatory ritual held by *all*.
Hunting was for many families a season-long affair. Moving
into their camps deep into the woods, all women, children,
horses, and dogs to hunt wild *hogs, deer, bear!* Uncle Henry &
The Boys hunted them *all*. There was Jimmy, Merlin, Bubba,
and me always after that *Big Ole Buck* to hang on the *wall*.

START SOMETHING NEW!

In sounding fathoms, deep common sound never heard
before, rings then fades into lyrical tingling sounds.
This parting vibration emitted from whence?
Holding dominance at which nothing compares or
shames; yet still withstanding an ever-present tone, held
in seclusion *hidden* behind and beneath a *Lonely Soul!*

MY CHILDHOOD

When as a child all that I knew was laughter, fun,
and play in the night as well as day, *No Fear* was on
my mind as curious things I would investigate.
No Worry of the morrow for food, and plenty
was bequeathed from *Nature's* hand.
With advancing from a child to a lad, this allowed one to
affirm their being was *not* what people of *Society* had.
As a child, calmness of *Love that I knew* is
The Thoughts of Childhood Days!

TIDE OF TALES

To be shared at a later date or never seen because of
money, it seems thoughts written down in candor and
jest, looking to be published for a posterity quest.
Thoughts derived from a person still alive seem
never to prevail. Others, whose works are *more* to the
point, step over others to reach *written success!*
Young adult or person in school may find *one day* this note of mine
not thrown away, trying to express feelings of *distress* in writing
profound thoughts, to me at least, and not being able to *add some
material to the Fire* when a young mind is set *Aflame* to read and learn!

TIDE OF TALES

To be shared at a later date or never seen because of
money, it seems thoughts written down in candor and
jest, looking to be published for a posterity quest.
Thoughts derived from a person still alive seem
never to prevail. Others, whose works are *more* to the
point, step over others to reach *written success!*
Young adult or person in school may find *one day* this note of mine
not thrown away, trying to express feelings of *distress* in writing
profound thoughts, to me at least, and not being able to *add some
material to the Fire* when a young mind is set *Aflame* to read and learn!

TO EDITOR
Riotous Risk in Today's Society

Owning, controlling *money* is means that controls this city's politics!
Where has beneficial media for betterment of/for *all*
to provide a sincere cause of better life gone?
In reading expressed opinions by politicians, name-calling,
finger-pointing, accusations made, much like children at play.
As an elderly person *50 and over* it seems that all of these
problems can be solved with a little forethought and
digression centered on a goal of helping the city, *not* certain
individuals that wish to benefit their own interest.
There are multiple areas that want to be used for an aboveground
multi-story parking garage, *but* who will benefit? Owner or public?
Just outside of the proposed Lightner area lie these places; i.e.,
the corner of May/San Marco Street, little links property,
and Riberia/King Street area, close *but* not too far away!
Who do these elected officials think they are? Certainly
no better than the people that elected them.
Graft and corruption will be exposed and that is when
somebody will need a lot of money *to buy their way out*!

THE FIG TREE

Standing *gaunt* and *full*, the fig tree sends forth a small
shoot on its many branches; therefore, shoots erupt
with flowers to grow into a tiny fruit of fig.
As growth permits, fruit grows round and
full, a moist, succulent fruit.
Birds appear to indulge with glutinous appetite.
Bright green leaves so large as to hide many different sizes of
ripe fruit on branches lounging underneath and inside.
Evening breezes in summertime cause leaves to *dance* and
frolic, while *bees* and *gnats* come to sample half-eaten figs.
A *lone* bull ant circles the tree to find *a meal* from what a *red wren*
leaves behind, nourishment derived from this *Fig Tree's Ale!*

THE OLD PLACE

Delicate roses on the fence *in front of Ancient Dwelling* cast
forth heavenly odorous scent that beauty carries!
Colors are unsurpassed enmeshed within sullen background
of green given to everything that grows in *Nature's Garden.*
Rain cascades forth over flowers below causing
them to *come alive* stand in beautiful show.
Honeysuckle vine also resides here with roses, lilies, and
ferns on or along the fence row in front of *Ancient Dwelling*
sending forth the *Heavenly Scent* only *Beauty* carries!

TABLE OF LORE!

Sitting at, talking about, same as reminiscing
through memories of the mind.
Laughing out loud, tears swelling from portals,
seeing the past so clearly *in your mind's eye*!
Table seating remembers bad ... *but good* most of all, without
scuff person involved is *you* standing tall above the rest!
Morsels galore of substance to eat to furnish *power* for you
to overcome this foe of when, where, why to live, partake
of willingness to overcome while seated at this *Table of
Lore* containing substance to eat that neither contains
calories or unwanted fat carved from *This Bull!*
As periods of time dispatch *seasons cradle* of innocence awash
in a gale of snow or maybe *laughing gale* notwithstanding
hurricane force, plentitude given to *big* guffaw requirements
are none for anyone sitting at this table to just have *fun.*
Serving is continued through the lifespan of woman *or* man, just sit
and *please* partake in ... remember when? Or that's just like before!
All consumed at this *Table of Lore!*

SONG OF MOSES

A quiet *thump* of the wagon ever constant, plod, clink of
traces in background singing of song birds, buzzing of
winged creatures, rising steam filtering through brownish-
black coat of *Moses,* mule that pulled and worked for men
who collected turpentine in *A Florida Pine Woods.*
Their *song* would begin each morn *long before dawn* would
awaken life's earthly inhabitants. Silent majestic star would
step forward onto the stage of life, dancing and singing
throughout bountiful forest greenery. Life's song, hard as
it was, would ring out in continuous harmony daily.
Perhaps forgotten today by those, who choose *not* to see, is the
Song of Moses forever engrained in Florida's pine woods history!

SUBJECT - HUSSEIN

Of this day for citizens concerned *to without delay* sally
forth with rampant revenge and eradicate hostility
from *Hussien!* Is fighting again required to *Vanquish
a foe* one who likes to spout threats and *stuff?*
Turn your back and walk away *but* carry a stick large
enough to *kill* the threat *if* and *when* it starts for real!
Neighbors of Iraq are held *to pay* if *they* let Saddam try
to have *his* way to isolate the nation of Hussein.
Then and only then will they fight among their
selves to erase a past from Death and Pain?
Bodyguards stand by to protect, like Noriega's. Are
they covert American CIA or Green Beret?
These are things that a select number are privileged to.
Are *you* one of those?

ROMANTIC JOURNEY

Time begins for the twain ever-spouting love extreme,
while others dream, and yet more just play to a
pair intertwined amidst star-crossed trails searching
for *their path* to follow accompanied
by a true friend speaks loudly, fervently, adding togetherness, peace,
understanding bequeathed by the two *on* this thing
called *Love* for *each other.*

ROSE GIVEN TODAY!

Flower growing free, *wild* like me, are not for few as the
rose I gave to you. Most illustrious thing to me is viewing
foliage that grows continually throughout Eternity.
Thinking that times of past supersede actions that took place this day.
The rose given to you is the rose that was the *same* given to
another for the same reason in another place on another day.
Actions of human style, demeanor, release Humanity's *Art of Love!*
Flowers given are words unspoken, meaning of which is in a person's
soul to which road of love delivers night and day around the globe,
never lost, just hidden away to be used another time, another day!
Meaning past, meaning today, assures your *soul* is here to stay!

MY COW DOG

Judy was about the right size, red with black patches here and
there. Sounds she made was a deep, beautiful *bawling echo bark*, a
sound that travels through the air and goes straight to your *heart*.
In the swamp, hunting cows, sounds of her baying a lone cow deep
in a palmetto thicket told this cowboy that *his job was starting*.
Yu could talk to your dog, she understood every word, so
that work moved along, cattle were rounded up, moved
into holding pens, this, with *help* from *Judy Dog*.
I *pioneer* told me one time *a cowboy* will have *maybe*
one good dog in his life, if he is lucky!
Days come and go! The sound of a cow dog
gives peace to a lonesome cowboy's *soul*!

RIDING HIGH TRAILS

Riding together along a serene mountain path, enjoying being
with your soul mate, one sees in your mind's eye that one need not
speak to understand your every thought and be with you *the same.*
Together means there is a feeling felt by both *that this is the right one,*
the one that life has led you to, the one both have been searching
for ... found there in the high mountain range of *The Rockies.*
As a child, your mind asks *"What will I be?"*
As a teenager, *"feelings"* lead the way.
Middle age says, *"What now?"*
Death, reborn, *start* all over again!
Living in high country, where air is thin and cold, causes a mind to
forget the past, just live for that day, *let tomorrow* take care of itself!

QUEST FOR LOVE

Riotous risk in reveling time emitted from ravenous serpent's tongue, glorious beauty propounded on starlight's gleam coming from a heavenly bright contagious smile.
These and only these fabricated *omen* that beckons unsuspecting travelers into yon *Temple* of *Love* with true maidens to serve beyond mortal thought to *your* delight and every whim of mind you have brought!
Travel light on this road of leisure, holding only respect for those before that trod so fervently. Trundle with peace on the journey's edge seeking truth on this quest *you* with movement swift as the eyes blink *a floral bouquet* have picked to *give you yon lass* awaiting in blissful happiness!

NET OF LOVE

Trying to reason when there is another is often not clear.
A *person in love* doesn't see *like you or me!*
Art of love is cast into the air to encircle a person's
heart and keep it there, as fishing on the beach when
you cast the net wide and far to trap the prey.
Two people in love *alike in most ways* brought together forever!
Compatibility will keep them and *neither one will stray!*

PELICANS

Where have all the Pelicans gone? Once they filled the
shoreline and sky, soaring so easily along on warm air currents
just above the wave line peering into the water below for a
school of traveling fish on which they would make a feast!
In my youthful days, while sitting on coquina rocks lining the
beach shore, these big, friendly birds would come sailing along in
groups of three or more while shrimp boats plied the ocean's shore.
Today ... where have all the Pelicans gone?
Human figures ply this beach shore now, enjoying *sun, fun,
play* never realizing that, because of them, Pelicans have gone,
as have other animals that forage for food retreat from man.
So where have all the Pelicans gone?

SEMINOLE WIND

Where I go without a care, bending a strain of life's piercing
air, *alone* needing someone, facing *truth* on *Seminole Wind!*
Air, it seems, is so clear high above in Mountain glen so fair,
Life's thread is drawn through *hills* or *valley's*
bend as you race astride *Seminole Wind!*
Love awaits there in Mountain's strain, learning
on *every* note of life's musical tone;
Every gleaming, lingering *note* played is so beautiful when
coming straight from *your soul* as I ride astride *Seminole Wind!*
Out of *smoke in the air* she appears as a ghost of tomorrow,
so fine and so fair, with *amber* painted eyes, coal black hair,
skin like lace: smooth, silky clean; a knowledge of *ages*
past held deep untold! To come forth only in certain ways,
nourishment for *that* day as I ride astride *Seminole Wind!*
Stories gathered through time are *never* lost when
set to rhyme; some truth, some likes, always there
forever like *shadows* after *Seminole Wind!*

THE BEACH

As a child plays in sand, water blue, ever so blue,
the old man travels through time thinking of days long past,
when in a flash, it was he in the same exact place.
Time has a way to repeat itself.
How is it when people, places, things, are not as *needed* as they were?
Do humans reach a certain point in life when
dreaded actions *no longer* take or require thought of or
apprehensions concerning fear of the former three?
Calm summer days require *call to unleashed humanity for* a full
day doing *utmost* to enjoy life! Digging worms, cutting a
long *witherly* cane pole with string and hook, an old coffee
can filled to the top with *dirty, night crawlers, bugs!*
You traipse casually off to the river. The art of fishing is to find a
secluded spot, a *honey hole*, where catching a lot of fish isn't important;
just being where *you* want to be *when* you want to be there! Letting
the world pass you, you don't even have to bait your hook.

RAPID DEMISE OF A FRIEND

Looking back isn't so bad when the future
stands directly in front of you.
The art of listening beget knowledge to which
no one tires, yet advancement of some leaves *truth*
naked and shorn estranged from you.

Night slowly retreats into day so then *truth* shall arise from ashes into
glorious light on a given day; alas, you arise facing foes in thought,
only realizing spirits in mind consume precious *time* leaving marks
deep bedded in hostility and hate for rapid demise of a *friend!*
Calling together some that care to love, never thoughts to humiliate,
only to emancipate dredging furrows from minds, freeing wealth
buried, holding back enormous rushes into never-quarried mountains
of knowledge, allowing rapid *growth* not *rapid demise of a friend!*

VICTORIA'S DELIGHT

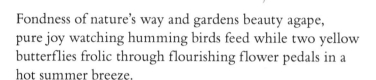

Fondness of nature's way and gardens beauty agape,
pure joy watching humming birds feed while two yellow
butterflies frolic through flourishing flower pedals in a
hot summer breeze.
Traveling down an old back-wood road, wild turkey appear
On this quite secluded patch of sand *dusting* their feathers before
Roosting for the night!
On a short way, a mother deer takes flight, disturbed
while teaching two yearling fawns *what to eat.*
Remembering time of travel through a *slough bay* when *jasmine*
Bloomed and, *oh*, the heavenly scent hanging in the air;
or collecting wild cabbage, palm dates, watching a Florida *panther*
on the marsh getting seafood to eat!
Florida born and raised, *Vicky's* happiness is in treasures that she
enjoys, day-to-day living where nature untouched is hers to
enjoy day and night.
That's *Victoria's Delight!*

WHITE BUFFALO

Passing of time will tell a tale of spring and the *White Buffalo*, child of days when means were lean seems shocked today when a person cannot dream, moons pass by, young turn old, sickness is overcome, yet a disappearing breed starts to return.
Time of the year when the *People* would hunt for meat that helped them survive a cold winter's chill or, perhaps, give clothing to wear all taken from the *Buffalos* hair and skin. Spirits told of a mighty thing when all men grew together as one, that peace to the world would come, children all would have food to eat, clothes to wear, and a place to sleep; all of these things will be assured when a *White Buffalo* appears to all.
Days are growing short, time lingers, still while the *Spirit* moves the *White Buffalo!* Look into the heavens for the sign of when the *Great Spirit* will allow the transformation of a windy storm to show a telling to come of *The White Buffalo*.

SONG OF RACHEL

Entering from the foyer with long, flowing, curly locks cascading
to her shoulders, this petite young female enhanced a bright and
energetic day on which I was passing in this particular way.
A certain gleam in her eye refreshed innermost depths of
my stagnated soul, happy thoughts everyone may enjoy!
Ah, youth and meanderings of a jay blend
together in a just and harmonious way.
Flowing of life's uninterrupted sway, traveling together
to live a distance away, as Mary and Joseph in seasons past
followed their hearts in life's never-ending quest.
Truth, Love, Happiness is bestowed upon the
twain forever in life, *two shall remain!*

WANDER LOST

Timber woods trails all seem alike,
even years alone as a child;
you did hike sensing to feel that
creatures who abound do, like eyes,
observing each step you make, trying
not to disturb a scene so peacefully quiet.
Chirp of a jay startled to see a creature
wandering lost, yet so contented, it seems.
A long babbling brook gives otters time to play
While frogs sign out in harmonious display.
Birds emit sounds that chime so fee while you
Wander in a wood, lost but *happy!*

THE BED OF

Things that register in mind to emit from voice have been said before
In another place from another's face. Before
is *now* and so on and so on;
History in place does again repeat itself only to gather for repetition in
Another's *space* or *race!*
What I think now has been thought before.
When past is brought forward, it all becomes new and so on and so on
as before; *turn it loose*, so it does not repeat.
Life accepts the lowest of beasts and thoughts.
Sounds will not change *sheets* in a bed of life after all!
So ... *Sing, My Brother, Sing!*

WILD BRONCO

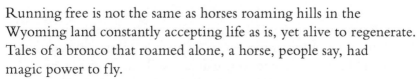

Running free is not the same as horses roaming hills in the
Wyoming land constantly accepting life as is, yet alive to regenerate.
Tales of a bronco that roamed alone, a horse, people say, had
magic power to fly.
Seen by few, but never doubted, was this horse of a different color
that raced across the mountain tops with fire flying from its hooves.
Time would tell if this *image* was true, for this tale was told around
campfires to little boys and girls of the *Sioux*.
Only a person with true heart and clear mind dare try to envision this
Magical theme, for unclean hands could never hope to see this
Magic horse in the sky or even in their dreams.
Children today have lost this dream, to be able to confront, touch,
ride a magic horse and to race over rivers and across mountains with
such speed and ease.
If only the *Wild Bronco* could be seen again!

THE GATOR HUNT

A Short Story by Sam Raven

Johnny Boy was working on his truck out by the oyster house
when I drove up, just coming out of the woods. Johnny spoke,
"David said he needed some baby gators; we'll put them in pens
with gator nests and tourists will think they *hatched*." He said,
"I know where some are that hatched down in the shores."
I said, "Yea, I know where that gator holes
is. How we gonna catch 'em?"
He said, "You got an old dip net? We'll shine 'em, then
slide the dip net under their tail, put 'em in the boat."
Johnny said, "Over there," pointing to a place by some
palmettos behind a house. On the ground was a net. He
picked it up and tossed it into the bed of his truck. Headlights,
battery was checked to see where *she-gator* was.
Getting to the marsh wasn't so hard. There were three ways
to get to a gator nest, so we went in by an "old dim" woods
road only locals and some hunters knew about that was
between Cedar Island Road and a large drainage canal.
After driving as far as we could, we walked an old
game trail, mostly used by wild hogs, deer, coons, a
black panther, and possum on to the marsh.
Walking along hog rail south, in black dark, point of
slough entrance was felt. The slough exited out of a little
hidden cove. A drainage canal fed from the head of this
slough and opened into this little hidden cove.
At a point where the canal entered the slough, a small creek
flowed coming out of the swamp. About 40 or 50 feet up that
creek was a mound built by a female gator. I found this perchance
one day while following my hounds when coon hunting.
Johnny turned on his light before entering the slough.
We had to find out where the female gator was at.
"Let's see if ole gator is on the marsh," Johnny said.
About 200 yards towards the intracoastal waterway,
there appeared two big red eyes looking at us.
Only words spoken were "There she is!"
Silently we moved toward the head of the slough. Before

taking a couple of deep breaths, we had entered a swamp
following the creek, stepping over fallen logs.
Johnny went around the edge stepping up on the *mound*
searching for baby gators. I walked straight toward *the mound*
and with one leap found myself crawling up beside of Johnny.
"They already hatched; let's look around this cove marsh."
Silent approach was made back into the cove. Standing a few
feet into the cove, Johnny searched by moving his headlight.
Four small red eyes were seen. He said to me, "There
are two over there. Let me go get 'em, okay?"
I handed him the dip net and silently he glided into the *black of night*.
After a while, he returned with two baby gators in his
hand, handing them to me. "I know where we might
be able to find some over in the next creek," I said. "If
not there, we can always got to Pellicer Creek!"
We gingerly returned to the truck, placing the babies
into a cooler with a little water for them to lay in,
and quietly left the marsh driving out of the area by a
different road that exited through the golf course.
A short drive south, we reached Dupont Center. Turning east
again, we travelled through the *hunt club*. Just before breaking
onto the marsh, we turned east and into the swamp underbrush.
Following an old logging road, one created by skidders, we
come to Moses creek-bank. Under shadows of water and
live oak trees, we slid the john boat into the water.
I sit in the rear so that when one is shined, I could paddle
the boat and maneuver it so that capture can be made.
Not traveling 50 yards, *red eyes* are spotted.
Johnny looks at me and, without a sound, points to the other bank.
I nod my head and turn the boat without a sound.
I put Johnny right on top of the gator with one fast sure motion.
Johnny turns around holding the gator, "Where we gonna put 'em?"
I said, "Just put 'em in the boat!"
Johnny laid the gator on the boat. It shot forward, crossed the center
console, jumped between my legs, and lay there for an instant.
I reached down, picked him up, and said, "I guess
we can tie him up with boot laces."
After catching a couple more, we decided to go home.
Next day, tourists visiting the gator farm would look down and
say, "Look at the babies. I guess they hatched last night!"

WISH OF A CHILD

Thoughts of my youthful days, carefree time
running through woods and underbrush,
hours spent camping or hunting deep into Florida swamps;
spending quality time with young offspring teaching
them to read tracks, to know *fowl and beast,*
fishing together, then cleaning and cooking a day's fresh-caught catch
over an outdoor fire in the woods or on the beach, *Oh, what a feast!*
I have always had a dog. Hounds, I find, are more
comparable to my lifestyle with woods and animals
that in surroundings live are a connecting link.
I pray that perhaps in my lifetime, living creatures will
not use and destroy plants or animals that maintain
or replenish things needed for humanity's life.
As a child, I remember *as evening shadows become longer* and
glow of dusk began to immerse everything into *black tone
of darkness*, a whistle would pierce the air looking toward
home, front porch lights would blink off and on.
Time to return to a quiet place of *warmth and love*, never thinking
of anything other than peace and protection found there *at home!*

A SUMMER DAY

Remembering the days of youth when you
and a friend would climb on your
Bicycle with a fishing pole and a coffee can full of fiddler
crabs, you ride to town to go fishing at the *Old Fort*.
Riding to the back of the Fort to sit on the seawall
to fish, the morning sun is sparkling in the blue-
green water of the bay so smooth.
The Park Ranger rides easily across the lawn on the mower that
is putting along at an even pace. The stillness is interrupted by
the sound of a lone mullet jumping in the water of the moat.
The coquina Fortress emits unseen memories of the
pat and holds scars of many battles past. Cannonballs
and round shot holes mark the path of man
The small ledge that circles the fort allows a person to
inch their way around the mighty structure. Under a
small slit window where Seminole leaders escaped from
imprisonment, your mind rushes wildly through time.
Around the fort, between the seawall and the east wall
of the Fort, stands an old fire oven that was used to
heat the cannonballs to fire at wooden ships.
Today the oven is used to burn trash. The afternoon is starting
to let the shadows extend and the tide has begun to turn.
The fish will start to bite. This is when you return to your favorite
fishing spot knowing that this is the time you will catch a fish
that you can take back home to Mom and say with a big smile,
"See what I caught?"

MOUNTAIN MIST

Smokey Mountain Call
Lingers indefinitely, causing mind to ponder past natural beauty
and abundance; contained therein sustains *life* - no more, no
less – modern convenience show people *what if* or *I want.*
Cherokee lived, planted, harvested *but* only took *what they*
needed from Mother Earth to live in harmony with nature.
Why has mankind *killed, maimed, corrupted* a people; so that they
could possess *gold*, a lesser metal, yellow in color, that men *kill for!*
Cherokee people believed that yellow color to be given
to corn, squash, beans, oranges, apples was *far* more
important *than that metal*, as did other nations!
You cannot eat it and it does not fill a man's stomach,
as does venison, squirrel, turkey, ducks, or fish.
It does not give the body strength, only ideas of
strength that causes corruption and death.
Death not of the body, but death of the soul and spirit,
leading to decay and causing the *ultimate death of the body.*
In *Mountain Mist*, life stands still. Senses awaken to sight,
sounds, smells, and touch of nature. *Pure Nature!*

ONE SPRING MORN

Sitting under Tall Cedar Tree on a warm spring
morn, out of the corner of my eye I catch movement
of a gray squirrel scurrying down a tree.
At the bottom, it pauses, its tail rapidly flicking
while it *tastes the air* with its nose.
After assurance, it hops through chain link fence and
begins to search the lawn for delightful treats.
A small reddish wren flies to tree. Out of *Loquat Tree*
steps a *Red Cardinal.* Two mocking birds sing melodious
verses as if to say *"Where are you? Where are you?"*
From powerline to powerline, another bird answers,
"Here am I. Here am I. But I am moving away!"
From an old dog pen comes chirping and tweets of small
birds, *gray with white* sashaying and screeching in and out
of neighbors plum trees during a bird food fight.
Oh, yes, what a treat to sit under Tall Cedar Tree on a
Warm Spring Morn to enjoy Nature's Delightful Show!

DAY THE DOG CAME HOME

'Twas much like any other late August day, sun beaming down
while black clouds were slowly forming in the southwest,
probably coming from islands in the Caribbean.
Looking back through fig, banana, loquat trees, a familiar sound
is heard, low, long, drawn-out bawl of your hound, head erect,
nose into the air, tasting the currents of the breeze, carrying scent
from afar, and you know from past experience to trust your dog far
more than your own senses, after all, the dog has proven himself.
Walking towards the dog pen, an 'ole friend appears
out of the cane break with tail erect, nose extended,
gleam in her eye, moving quickly, silently.
Bryan's other hound comes to the pen.
Feeding time at the old backwoods Florida homestead!

CATTY MOUSE SLOUGH

Time passes by and through memories of mind
in days when I thought *only of you.*
Waters run deep in a back water slough,
places we fished together, *me and you.*
Days gone past never to re-appear again
are days lived on *Catty Mouse Slough.*
A *Creole* woman was a friend, Suz:
dark eyes, cold black hair, with love so true,
In her Daddy's perot on the black water slough
She would come to me by the light of a moon.
Fishing together made me laugh, when reeling
in a big mouth bass, a scream of delight would
pierce the air, knowing that only she and I were there.
Love in her dark eyes was there to see, a tender
sweetness, her lips gave *to me* thoughts
taken from a back water – give never-ending
meaning to the *Catty Mouse Slough!*

FLOWERS

I planted some flowers yesterday in hopes they will enlighten
a happy way for any person taking a walk
through God's garden of peace.
Shamrocks from Ireland planted so true,
to brighten a world that's blue
and maybe a little bit of added *luck* while passing will rub off on you!

On top of the southeast part of the hill, a handful of Hosta is planted
to grow for a tropical atmosphere. Behind
the fish pond, just a little west
of the waterfall, a few giant blue hostas lay,
with rich natural dirt all around,
given energy to grow, large and beautiful one day soon will astound.

Being last to go into a raised perfect bed are *garden*
huckleberries. These, too, will be good to eat, after momma
makes a jam that goes with biscuits, bread, or meat.
Tomatoes are filling and tasty, too, planted in time down in the
low part of the yard. With grace and thought, a little work, too,
Heaven on Earth can be found in this, God's garden of peace.

CHRISTMAS IN ST. AUGUSTINE

'Twas the night before Christmas, when all through the town,
no roses were frozen, no snow fluttered down.
No children in flannels were under the trees,
shortened pajamas were all you could see.
To find wreaths of holly was not very hard,
for holly trees grew in most every yard.
In front of the houses were daddies and moms,
Admiring their shrubbery and coconut palms.
The excited kiddies were giggling with glee,
In hopes they'd find water skis under the tree.
They all knew that Santa had come a long way,
Driving his convertible instead of a sleigh.
They all knew he had come and done his work,
without even a second to linger or shirk.
He whizzed up the highways and zoomed down the roads,
in his shiny new sports car, delivering his loads.
The tropical sun was about to glow,
and Santa knew it was time to go.
As he jumped from his car, he gave a wee chuckle;
he was dressed in Bermudas with an ivy league buckle.
There were no chimneys, but that caused no gloom,
For Santa came through the Florida room.
He stopped at each house, but stayed only a minute,
And emptied his bag of the things he had in it.
And before he departed, he treated himself
to a glass of papaya juice left on the shelf.
Then he turned with a jerk and bounced back into his car,
remembering he still had to go very far.
But I heard him exclaim as he went on his way,
"Merry Christmas St. Augustine, I wish I could stay!"

HOLE

What is a *Hole?* Something created, dug, formed, or
perhaps imagined in a person's mind; depth of which is
untold, endless cavern of thought hidden from all.
Ancient times tell of things to come, time is here for man to
see things predicted are but a few; time for mankind to start
history anew instead of returning to days of old, but to use ideas
created in time with movement of earth and days gone by.
These things are not lost or buried in a *hole*, but are alive in someone's
mind brought out at the right time to enlighten the human soul!

SENSING

To light the night with evening stars to
pave the way for heavenly bliss,
these things were done for humanity's awareness.
The beauty of a lone soaring eagle gliding effortlessly thru the air,
the chatter of a squirrel high in a tree, the
smell of the wet meadow grass
after a brisk summer evening rain, these things
God provides for you and me.
The love of man for Mother Earth has long
been one of comprehension,
the love of Home, Hearth, and Nation.
The beauty of the one that you hold so dear,
the smell of a new babe that you clasp so near,
the calm voice in the time of fear,
that relieves the tension and belays the fear.
To walk in heavenly love and light, humanity
never should dread the dark of night.
In times when all seems lost, at quiet times when you count the cost,
this is when you live to find the life that you thought you lost.
Like the eagle, you spread your wings to fly,
so treetop high as the rain blesses the dry earth,
you do the same with the tears you cry.
The beauty that you contain in your heart and mind
is the thing that everyone searches for and never can seem to find.

SAILING

Seagulls floating on the clear endless sky,
wind wisping over an ocean ever so blue,
touching your raven hair so soft and light
on a day that is for sheer delight.

Two people together in love see things in different ways,
all is right in love scenes of the day.
Skimming effortlessly across the waves,
our boat of love travels on its way.

The air fills the sails, driving the vessel on.
The breeze is strong and full, like one's heart
filled with love for the one you hold so dear;
this, too, is your reason for carrying thru.

As the weather changes, so does the delicate line of life;
some are castaways, others find dry ground and the
everlasting love of a true husband and wife.

My boat is sailing this ocean so blue,
the sails are filled with the breeze so true.
Whatever happens is left to fate,
the one I search for is a true, loving mate.

A lone bird circling overhead tells the story of
Love, Laughter, and Life left to fate:
One and only one that is left after losing their mate.
Alas, I can no longer endure the solitude of life so bare.

I have a picture in my mind's eye of the one that is waiting for me on
distant shores or a beach close by.
I trim the sails on the vessel so bright.
Never mind the search for the one that is *right*.

A GARDEN OF LOVE

The garden is blessed with life-giving rain
to grow, produce, and produce again.
The circle of life is seen year to year,
throughout the seasons, life mysteries are made clear.

Spring, summer, winter, and fall,
life's circle is expressed in them all.

Life's freedom is brought to mind in a garden!
The different plants grow harmonious.
In this tremendous splendor of flowers and scent,
the unseen non-harmonious foliate is prevalent.
To these are drawn creatures of life:
the butterfly, birds, earthworms, slugs, and bugs.
The beauty of life is *Together all things survive.*

The tall pines stand straight and tall, as lone sentinel
to protect the evergreen growth below.
Oak, hickory, cedar are but a few of the many trees
blended together as a buffet to protect the tender
undergrowth that we see and know.

Blue jays, ravens, thrushes galore, honeybees, yellow fly,
Snakes and frogs.
These are but a ration of things that gather around and on
the garden's *old rotten log.*

The water feature is the mainstay for tadpoles,
goldfish, fly and their larvae.
The sound of the waterfall calls birds together.

The sweet scent of many different wild flowers, roses,
lavender, honeysuckle, and buttercup causes the mind
to mellow and drift away in light airy bliss.
All of this is brought to reality when the one that you love
caresses your face and touches your soul with a tender kiss.
The garden of love is eternal and forever,
In this splendor, I long to live, and leave it.

THE FLORIDA COWBOY

Friendship cannot be seen or heard, only feelings delivered
through a kind word and space.
The friendship of two apart and unseen lingers forever;
not to decrease, but to grow to infinity.
To receive a gift from a friend is to add to the collection of
memories contained in one's storehouse in the mind.
The unraveling day is brought to mind when the thought
of early morning appears through the cypress trees.
Slowly moving cattle trudge down an old dusty,
rickety road that goes through the boggy bay and will
end up at the cattle pen on Tillman's Ridge.
The horse and dog are the only friends that the Florida
cowboy has or wants. The calmness of being alone in nature
with your best friend and your constant companion is
accomplished through a gentle touch, whistle, or motion.
The horse, a constant companion, and the dogs are your best friends.
Nature is the ultimate work of art created by
the *Great Spirit* known to you and me!

IN THE PINE WOODS

Born in St. Augustine town, in the county of St.
Johns, on the banks of the San Sebastian, the home
was on Spanish Street in the heart of the town.
At the age of three, the city was left, and residence was made on the
Dessilberger Estate on *Old Spanish Trail*.
From this homestead, within an hour or two walking time,
the Seminole Chief Osceola was taken captive, under a flag
of truce, and brought to the small village of St. Augustine.
As a boy running in and hunting the back woods,
fishing and swimming in Moultrie Creek, we often
rested by the stone monument, with the bronze
emblazoned plaque, in the back pine woods.
This area, known only to the hunters, was
simply called *The Monument*.
Today, the only thing protecting this from encroachment
by the ever-growing population of humanity are the
woods that are owned by the timber company.
About a quarter of a mile north where Ft. Parton was
located is a park for recreation and homes to live in.
Laughter from children come from under those trees
where history states that violence once, back in time on
this very spot under these same trees, did take place!

THE HUNT

Before the sun peeks its bright, shining head through the
early morning mist, you slip out of the back door *gun in
hand*. After putting the gun in the truck's rack, mustering
all of the body's strength, you lift the dog box into the
truck. They become excited in the pen and want to go.
With much hollering and cussin' at the dogs, you call
them by name and gingerly load them into the box.
With a hot cup of coffee, you jump in the truck and start for
the swamp. Casting the dogs to jump a deer, is done with
glee, hoping that today will be the day when you bag that big
old mossy-antlered *big buck deer*, the one that will be featured
in "Woodsmen Magazine," or maybe it will be "Boone &
Crocket," the book established for a champion deer.
The horse is unloaded with the dogs. They start out on the saw
grass flats traveling from cypress island to cypress island.
Midway the dogs get a scent, the pace is quickened. The dogs enter
an island and a deer emerges from the back. The race is on! The man
on horseback runs past the dogs. The deer is fast and runs real low.
The deer, horseback rider, and dogs in hot pursuit
all disappear into the settling mist.

THE TALKING WINDS

They are unseen, screaming, crying, and moving silently
through the forces contained in and on Earth.
These forces move and sculpt the crust of
this planet that mortals live on.
The seas move the earth and care passages.
Unseen, only felt, this force is called *wind*.
Sailing, surfing, flying a kite; the wind talks, the one
that hears is the one that is in touch with the earth.
To be aware, the wind will talk to you, whistling through
a deep canyon or howling in mighty gusts, driving on a
storm, the quiet whisper, high in the mountain hollow.
Across the ancient sands travels the hollow
whirling dervish of the *sand devils*.
The winds are talking in different tones and ways, always talking.

SALT RUN OYSTERS

When you are born in St. Augustine, Florida, you know the place to harvest saltwater oysters is behind Conch Island down in Salt Run.

Today Conch Island and the south end of Salt Run are a State Park. Directly across the north of the lighthouse, the Ponce family has homesteaded, declaring old Spanish land grant priority relating back to Ponce de Leon.

The Indian tribes that were living in this area once relied on these oysters to stay alive. Today pollution from the populace, the use of motor boats, sewage, and fertilizer runoff has hurt salt run.

With time, however, nature will prevail; Salt Run will regenerate itself and there will be delicious big oysters to harvest once again.

THE SECOND TIME

The one for me
is someplace you see ever hiding
and playing so coy, always alive, smiling, full of joy.
The time will come
for me and she, but as for now,
I carry on free as the hawk, alone as the wolf.
The kids are grown
and starting lives of their own.
The time is easy and no more do I rush, for you see,
the things that were dreams are old and full of rust.
The things of youth
no longer do I need, it's peace
and quiet with a loving mate, I plead!
Fast horses, liquor,
and bar girls are the things I no longer want
or need, but the love of a good, beautiful wife,
that is my true friend indeed.

REMEMBER WHEN

Passing the time from adolescence to being an adult.
Can you remember when the exact time that this occurred?
The time when games and playthings that were the
most important thing in your life were no longer *that* interesting;
when your buddy and friend no longer joined in a
good ole mud ball fight, but liked to stay clean
and remain in the house?
You always knew that she was a girl, but what goes on here?
Why doesn't she enjoy exploring the woods and swamp,
setting a trap line, and checking it every day,
or just doing nothing and setting on the bank of the stream
trying to catch a fish or digging worms for bait?
Why don't girls realize that all of those things are *great*?
Instead of fast pitch *hardball*, they like to play *softball* ...
Slow pitch, by the way.

HAPPY MOTHER'S DAY

Family

Like the peas in a pod, always together,
side by side, arm in arm, wrapped as one family;
each one from its mother's seed,
all the same, yet still individual.
With God's power and strength,
it will have the same chance at life as its elders have had
to grow strong and bloom with the rest of the peas.

Happy Mother's Day!

Love Ya, Bryan Goode

ONE SPRING DAY

I was sitting on the front porch of the old back woods rustic
home one dreary, hot spring day. The temperature was in the
nineties; a day so hot and muggy that the blooming flowers and
shrubs all folded their leaves and drooped their branches.
The sky was showing some movement of clouds coming from the
southeast. The wind picked up into a hasty, arrogant, crispy swirl.
Moisture could be sensed through my sunburned broken nose.
The facial scars, broken nose, the acquired back in '67 during the
Viet Nam War, the sense of rain is felt and tasted in the air. A
big black thunderhead crosses the sky and small drops are felt.
In the sky, bolts of finely bright, bluish-green and silver-gray
electrical charges erupt. At the same time, deep sounding
ominous groans of ominous thunder come forth.
The dogs are frightened and try to come into the house. The
rain is falling in sheets by this time! Everyone seeks shelter: the
birds, squirrels, cats and dogs find a warm, dry place to rest
quietly and enjoy the cooling relief of this *spring afternoon rain*.

PICTURE IN MY MIND

I wander alone thru the endless foliage of my mind,
seeking to find the one Angel that can calm the raging
torrent, never-ceasing to allow me the true love and beauty
of the one siren I see constantly in depths of my mind.
Out of the shadows she appears: black hair, dark eyes, glistening skin.
Into the depths of my soul she looks, always aware of the emptiness.
To love one endless thought in mind, soul, and body; alike
but different, together but apart, always knowing,
struggling to reach the unseen apex of the ladder of life,
to achieve supremacy over the things that one dreads.
Behold, the signs of earthly days,
are they not the same as eons past?
Humanity continually tries to change.
The earth does not.
In your game of life, how will you cast your lot?

MY FRIEND TIANA

French and German were the only sounds that she
heard from the gentle women who cared for *abandoned*
children speaking only their native tongue.
At seven months of age, she left the orphanage, traveling
from Viet Nam and arriving in the United States.
The years of adolescence were extremely hard, filled with
learning. Entering adulthood, the years were far more intriguing.
Leaving home and hardship, she entered military life.
Through years of stress, strain, wars, and pain, the strength
of body and mind grew. Returning home and entering the
civilian workforce almost cost her life. A truck accident
on a mountain road almost accomplished what two wars
could not! Unconsciousness and death were not listed in
the Book of Life being printed for this time and place.
To tell a tale of love so true is but a fantasy of life that is bold and
blue. Leaning on memories of past stories that cannot be told;
stories of endless day and nights when stars were so clear and
bright in a jungle setting that only you know. The days with you
were not the same as the death, blood, and pain; only in a *secret*
war with people that do not have a name, there for a mission,
and then they disappear never to be revealed or seen again.
Like a kitty that chooses a person to love, the same is for
mankind when two people let their *hearts* entwine.

THE BOAT THAT DIDN'T FLOAT

In a person's mind, a thought is transferred from side to side.
In life, two people apart must devise a way to get together
when there is a river between the two.
One on this side, the other across the way,
with water in the middle, a boat must be made.
A boat to cross the watery moat,
a sturdy boat that will float the moat.
Time and timber will be had to build the sturdy boat
that will float across the vast watery moat.
The boat was built and ready to go.
People climbed aboard the sturdy boat that was built
to cross the vast watery moat to get to the other side.
The moment came to cast off from shore
to get to the other side.
In doing so, it was soon found that *the sturdy boat* built
to cross the vast watery moat was a sturdily built boat
that did not float!
Alas and alack, there can be no turning back.
A flotation device was quickly made
and across the vast watery moat, the people did float
and, thus, the journey was made.
Two people in love can find a way
to cross the angry seas.

GIFT OF MONEY

Money, money, money galore;
Lots of money you gave to me,
now I want more!

The gift was made so a child would not need
but now the gift given has turned to greed.

The gift given from the heart
is given so a person may have
a fresh start.

Too much money freely given to an unappreciative person
is like feeding fodder to an *ass.*

When it is eaten up,
there is nothing but wind to pass;
and talk is cheap when *you're full of gas.*

MOM'S HOT SAUCE

The relish of Hell is a succulent treat,
a most desirable condiment to eat,
using natural herbs and spices, you must not delete
the Minorcan datil pepper, for after completion,
it does compliment fish, fowl, and meat.

Ida Solana, most noted homemaker, wrote down the ingredients she
used so the people would not forget *that bottled Hell was delicious to eat.*

You gather palmetto fans, weave them into a hat, then
place a pint mason jar *full of relish* in the middle of that.

Give this as a gift and you will always, with much relish,
be invited back.

THE WILD COW HUNT

Lawrence's cattle busted out of the back pasture
fence which bordered Uncle Gus's hunt club.
After years running wild and grazing on *Wolfe
Ranch pasture*, I was asked to round them up.
With the help of Alton and Ray, we loaded horses, dogs, and ropes;
then with four-wheel drive trucks, departed for 12-Mile Swamp.
The first three days was trailing and looking for cattle, roping,
tying up, pulling single, rogue bull yearlings and horned cattle to
a central point where I would bring the goose-neck stock trailer.
On the third day, a bad little short-horned bull was
in the middle of a large palmetto thicket.
When the two cowboys went in after him, he hooked the horses and
time had to be spent doctoring the horses and letting them heal.
Days passed by, then we stared out early one foggy spring morning.
The cattle were feeding in the *Wolfe pasture*. With dogs and horses,
cattle were rounded up, cow dogs kept them in a circle.
Herding the cattle across the road into the catch pen was
accomplished and the wild herd of cattle was no longer a problem.

YOUR MIND'S EYE

Visual guides every day that leads a person down *life's*
ragged way is to be suspended in time aligning yourself
with famous or the infamous and general humanity.
A mind is the window of a powerful vehicle
transporting someone anywhere, anytime!
Landing of a bird on a limb in front of you, many bright,
beautiful butterflies alighting on colorful flowers, the brook
that wanders, meanders lazily along happily bubbling over
rocks, stones, and carelessly falling over sheer walls, only
to gather itself together at the base to flow on again.
Nature still is an untamed force that mankind tries to
emulate and stimulate, but cannot quite get it *right*.

WHAT IT IS?

Love, true love that is alive forever,
not simulated or faked;
the kind of thing that brings all of your senses awake.
The feelings and sensual pleasures of knowing
the exact thing to say at
the exact moment it is needed or,
perhaps, doing something like making *a good cup of coffee.*

The love of two betrothed that stands the test of time
is truly admired by all.

A marriage will in time be tested.
How many will survive and who will fall?

At times the fallen can start over again.
How many times have marriage vows been broken?

The vows *to forsake all others* and *until death do us part*
is not written to be spoken without true love
that will forever stay in your heart.

AS IT WAS TOLD TO ME
A Short Story By: Lester Goode

The early days in Florida were, at that time, pretty sparse. Take Jacksonville, for instance, mostly working-class people. St. Augustine back then was the playground for the rich and famous.

Grandpa Leth lived in the last home on the beach from Jacksonville Beach to Vilano Beach. Mom, who was the first born of thirteen children, was her daddy's helper, as well as helping her mother around the house.

Over in Palm Valley, lived the Mickler, Oesterreichers, and a couple of other German families. At this period in history, prohibition was in effect. Mom and Dad were in the horticulture business, gathering flowers, palm fronds, ferns, etc., for the florists in Jacksonville.

Poppa Leth also made his own wine. In the back of the *big house* was a barn where the horses, goats, and hogs, plus pigs lived. Beside the barn were milking platforms for the goats that ran wild.

Every day, Mom had to milk the goats. She would tell that there was one billy goat that she was afraid of because he had *big* horns, and he would attack you and knock the fire out of you. When milking time came, she used different tricks to trap him so he couldn't get close to her.

One time Mom and her brothers enticed their sister Tilley to ride one of the horses. *Ole Dan* was a retired racehorse. Then Tilley finally got on the horse's back, one of the boys took a Spanish Bayonet leaf and stuck the horse in the rear. *Ole Dan* took off like a shot. Through the sand dunes and down the beach went the horse with Tilley holding on screaming.

One day when riding down the beach in the back of the horse and wagon, Mom jumped out of the wagon to do something and sprained her foot. Back in those days, cattle ran free and would come out of the woods onto the beach. With a child having a swollen, sprained foot, the only thing to do was to take immediate action. Grandpa used his own form of medicine. The thing to use to relieve such an injury would be heat, moisture, and relaxing on a soft bed.

At this time, Mom was told to sit down on
the beach and emerge her hurt
foot into a big fresh pile of cow dung. Crying
out "Daddy, don't make me
put my foot in that." The method was crude, but effective.

AS IT WAS TOLD TO ME
A Short Story By: Lester Goode

I still remember when Mom told about the time her dad had his crew down in the Guano, so she had to drive the horse and wagon down into the area where they were working to take lunch. About halfway into the Guano, a bunch of wild hogs and pigs ran out of the bushes and were between the horse's legs and under the wagon blowing, popping their gums. It was all she could do to hold the horse, to keep him from running away.

As I previously stated, this was *prohibition time*. People made moonshine and it was hard to go into the woods, unless people knew who you were and why you were there.

There are many stories and tales that people talk about when remember with old friends. Most of all, the old-timers that were involved with that sort of thing are either too old or dead.

The money that they made is still being used by their offspring. If you know their names, then you know
where their money came from.
A lot will die holding onto their secrets.

As for me, I just stay to myself, shake my head, and laugh when some young person asks *remember when?*

You can bet, I knew where things were kept and *the truth!*

THE TRANQUIL PERIOD OF FALL

The turning of the leaves is a quiet calm beautiful sight.
The many different fall colors do not appear overnight.

Day by day, greens turn to gray, browns to yellow,
and purple to orange, floating, wafting,
ever so gently to the ground.

The birds and the squirrels rustle through moss,
gathering nuts to stock away to use again on a
snow-covered wintry day.

Under ground a tunnel can be found,
a maze through the garden for the little
ground mole crickets that here abound
create fine fete for a ground mole.

In air busy flight is the buzzing of the bee,
moving from flower to flower, pollinating all of the
flowers and citrus trees,
consuming their nectar to transport back to
their home so honey can be made.

Under a citrus tree, a frog has made his home
deep in the earth where it will be safe and warm.

These are but a few of the things that are found
in the *Tranquil Period of Fall.*

TRUNDLE OFF TO BED

Darkness draws neigh, winter winds sigh.
Logs burning in the fireplace crackle emitting flames of glee
while sounds of snapping pop up a chimney does flee.
Movement outside foretells of snow on the way!
Animals all, big and small, hurry to scurry and locate
homes made in secret caches built for safety, food, warmth
from winter's deadly fare.
As you nestle in bed with book in hand,
so nimbly pages turn with grace and speed,
time passing so fast,
you trundle off to bed.
In deep nightly slumber, dreams elusive seem to appear
passing through time, back in childish years,
good times then back when.
How time misplaces thought often remembered,
but never lost: places, people, things steeped in time
are *dreams* after *you trundle off to bed.*

TO THINK!

The early crisp morning that you once recall
when you sat alone on the sand dune and
watched the sun slowly rise from the calm endless sea,
climbing high in the sky, coming from the east
and ever so gently settling in the west.
Hearken, the wind blows strong and crisp.
The course of life is free and clear to see,
but the game of life is mean and tough.
Life goes on and life passes by.
The realm of a person's mind is long and wide,
the venture to escape is often found to be never-ending and evasive.
The trip through time is brought to bear through age.
Growing, learning, living, these three things
are repeated over and over again,
never to stoop, yet always to remain.
Life is a mystery to a young person's heart.
The music of life turns into a symphony in later years,
a different tune from the one heard at the start.
The fast beat is succumbed by an even leisurely pace.
The often overlooked particles of life now
arise and become more profound ...
The hidden beauty that is so often passed by cries out,
"Here am I!"
Open your eyes and fill your heart.
Breathe in deeply filling your lungs, at the
same time filling your mind.
The world is but a place for one to house the human race.
Wisely used, it will last forever.
Wrongfully used, humanity's future is destined for untold schemes,
ones that live in the land of dreams.

THOUGHTS

To write words in rhythm and rhyme
with beautiful meaning related to the time.

The art of verse is oft misunderstood.

In dire times of greed and need, a person's thoughts
are written to feed the spacious rooms of the hungry brain
to store away and be used again.

The thoughts delivered to you through channels of mire
are thoughts that are learned, boxed, to be recalled at your desire.

At times misplaced, but never lost;
to be retrieved again
when needed the most.

BY: Lester Goode

TIME

I often think of you and I wonder what life has awarded you,
if you are happy?
I think of penguins and kitties, and your face
flashes into my mind, should I write?
Or must I leave everything behind.
The distance of mind is but a microsecond of thought.
The idea of time travel is but to close your eyes;
Instantly you travel to any point of your life,
the tender moments or the horror of *bad times*.
The future is but a journal. Each day is a page for which
you do not know the ending.
Ah, the one who wrote the book knows the ending,
also the place and time.
Personally, every day is to be lived with
love, honesty, shame, and hope.
The journal of life is endless, so many chapters
and verse, so much to learn.
Will we succeed?
The answer is self-contained, only you will determine the ending.

TIANA

Weaving the web of unseen mystical threads of never-ending love,
the all knowing, ever beautiful *Golden Female* accepts her given fate;
like the butterfly fluttering endlessly from
flower to flower, gathering nectar and
plating spores so that plants will flourish and
renew their image once more.
Each living thing has a *Golden Female*;
in her own way and times she will master her given destiny
like the trees, flowers, snakes, birds, and bees.
The dance of life is to a wonderful tune; the way
that you dance is the tune that you hear.
Water flowing from a clear mountain stream is
harmony and love that comes from above.
The beautiful female smiles constantly!
The Colorado Rockies are her home in the sky;
with clear blue water and loving friends, life
goes on in a never-ending pace.
Life is filled with love, beauty, and grace.

THE FOX HUNT

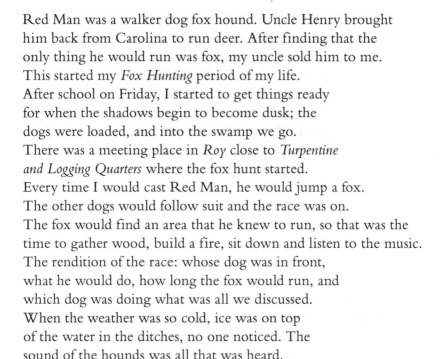

Red Man was a walker dog fox hound. Uncle Henry brought
him back from Carolina to run deer. After finding that the
only thing he would run was fox, my uncle sold him to me.
This started my *Fox Hunting* period of my life.
After school on Friday, I started to get things ready
for when the shadows begin to become dusk; the
dogs were loaded, and into the swamp we go.
There was a meeting place in *Roy* close to *Turpentine
and Logging Quarters* where the fox hunt started.
Every time I would cast Red Man, he would jump a fox.
The other dogs would follow suit and the race was on.
The fox would find an area that he knew to run, so that was the
time to gather wood, build a fire, sit down and listen to the music.
The rendition of the race: whose dog was in front,
what he would do, how long the fox would run, and
which dog was doing what was all we discussed.
When the weather was so cold, ice was on top
of the water in the ditches, no one noticed. The
sound of the hounds was all that was heard.
Nothing else mattered outside the dark, isolated
swamp and the music of the *Fox Hounds*.

THE DREAM

A young man's belief in his country is great.
When the call comes to go to war, he doesn't hesitate.
He gives his all without any qualms during
the conflict, his beliefs are changed.
The things that he would die for are no longer estranged.
Life is worthless, no one cares.
Does this foretell of things to come?
The life we lived, the happiness we shared?
Is this to be sold for the prospect of silver and gold?
The food we eat today is but a small point to consider.
In ages past and the future ahead,
where will it come from and who will be fed?
A weaver of words, a spinner of time once
penned a verse in eloquent rhyme,
"Silver or gold is not a gift, only an excuse for a gift.
A true gift is when you give of yourself love, true love."
The love of one's God, country, self, and mankind
are but a start for the future of time.
In all, things working together ensures surviving.
Can mankind survive? Or die trying?

THE SWAMPS

The calmness, peace, sounds that are found
on the edge of a marsh creek bank or in the heart of a swamp,
all of these places are untouched by humanity;
man is accepted by the residing animals as just another animal.
The only common thing is food, not money.
The conflict erupts when a human animal takes
the other *wild animal's* food or fishing/hunting place.
As the old saying goes, "You take mine, I'll take yours."
The indigenous animals will share with man.
Man can only take *for the sake of silver or gold*
to build or to have something before we die.
Is it too late to not build for *prosperity*
or is all former just a lie?

SUZANNE'S POINT OF LIGHT

The strength of your unlimited will is brought to light by a fountain.
The sparkling, gushing, bubbling spray that emanates
proceeds to influence the human's thought!
As the actions of the airy bubbles transfixes memory,
the actions of mortals repeats the latter.
When you marry, the presence of taste and smell are
enhanced to the ultimate.
The state of body and mind are referred to as *being in love.*
The longing to be with one and only one takes place!
The action of an animal is to smell.
This is programmed in the mind. It is either likeable or unsatisfactory.
What are your thoughts pertaining to this subject?
Are you a fountain or just an airy bubble?

MA MA

In casting my eye on the things that I see
in my heart, I wish to relate these things in my
mind, body, and soul from me to thee.
Aha, you say these things are here,
but the words do not come so easily.
The timing is right, but the flow?
It just don't go!
One day you just wait and see,
the words, they will come more easily.
The flow will go like the turning of the tide
on a clear spring morn when the turning of the earth
lets the movement flow so smooth,
it's almost like molasses moving down the sides
of a fresh stack of blueberry hotcakes.
When you read what is said, it will fill your mind
like homemade bread;
the kind Ma Ma would make,
and the scent flowing through the air out the back door
would bring you running to beg for the first end piece.
Oh, that covered in jam, what a feast!
Ya know *life doesn't get any better than this!*

THE MOCKING BIRD

The Mocking Bird, *gray and white*, sings so softly
and is elegant in flight.

Whether perched in a tree or perhaps sitting
on a fence rail close to me.
The beautiful sounds this creature makes is truly *Heaven Sent.*

Two Mocking Birds on the front lawn zip and whip through the air.
After this acrobatic show, each decides the way they must go.
One atop the chain link fence, the other in the grass
looking for insects to eat.

Looking aloft in the distant sky,
a formation of six fly wingedly by.

The shadows are long and the evening sky is sullen and gray.
Is this to foretell of rain on the way?

The birds sense something and fly ahead
so that when the rain descends,
the Mocking Birds will be in a safe, dry place.

After the shower, others appear. The Blue Jay emerges as if to say
"The rain is gone, come out and play."

The Cardinal flies in with his *Red Hen.*
A big, pretty black Woodpecker lands on the old oak tree.
Four Dove land on the telephone line.

Over all of this, the Mocking Birds reign *supreme!*

GLADES

The sounds that rise from the Everglades,
the flyway of many bids such as the osprey,
whooping and hook-bill crane.

The ducks and song birds, butterflies abound,
the sand fleas and fiddler crabs are alive on the creek banks
and on the flat marsh ground.

The egrets were so many at one time that the sky
was blocked when they would fly.

The man and the shotgun put an end to that,
for the money that they would not deny.

Now the sand hill crane can be seen in their flight
honking high in the sky as they fly by.

The turtle, fish, and alligator all live together;
the snakes, frogs, and stinging mosquitoes there abound.

High atop an old cypress tree is a nest built by the *Bald Eagle*;
The fish hawk flies above the water seeking its daily meal.

One of the clowns of the swamp plays
and swims nearby; the otter is as much at home
on land as in the water.

Life in the Everglades, home of the Seminole!

MAKING HAY

Down in the meadow one early spring,
the sun starts to appear and the dew frogs sing.

Up at the barn, the tractors roar to life,
different machines are hooked up with a clanging metal ring.

The day has started and the hay baling will begin!

Two Olivers and one Allis-Chalmers emerge through the gate;
one will mow, one will set, the other will rake;
at about ten or so, no one will take a break.
At twelve, everyone goes up for lunch.

After lunch, the Vermeer round boiler is hooked up and charged.
Returning to the meadow, the bailing will start.

The weather controls all on a farming operation
on a cattle ranch *so fine.*

One thing for sure, *you can't make hay if the sun don't shine.*

LA GRACE ANNA

The old city is but *remains* from days long past
when people were elegant
and grace with charm
were developed, not acquired.

Days of long past dreams being developed
into reality still remain
in the soil of ancient ruins.

The one thing that cannot be returned is the love;
the love of health, wisdom and wit;
the love of a cool summer night when the
breeze floated across the glistening bay,
caressing the features of the one that you hold so dear;
the soft cooing of the whip-poor-will,
the full yellow moon shining so bright,
the ease of mind and the glow of your heart.

These are the things that make a man want to have a wife,
one to share these feelings and share your life.
The thought is there *only in your mind*.
The only things missing are the girl, the place, and the time.

THE MAGIC WOMAN

If I could only see you now!
The love I feel when you are around is
strong and forever will abound!
The rhythm and the music of a heart filled with love
fills the outermost realm of the desert of loneliness.

The tone of your voice soothes the strong seas of depression
and calms the uncertain waters of the unknown.

Laying beside you simply fills my body with the strength that is
achieved with the attitude of finding the one that is made *Just for me!*

Who is she, where is she?
Like the *Black Magic Woman*, playing games with someone's
feelings of the heart.

A love potion that turns a man's head, a subtle
glance from captivating eyes, the wisps of heavenly
scent that sends a man's brain totally *insane.*

To hold her, to touch her silk-like smooth
skin, your eyes lock with her eyes.
This is when she has you under her spell, not your will to be done,
but hers!

Ah, the pleasure that a wife gives to her husband
and the husband to his wife,
Simply stated are *Love, Life, Laughter!*

TO KNOW YOURSELF

Relationship with God,
to believe in The Christ
in written words taught by man
exclaims that one is created in the
image of God.

In being so made, is not one the same as one;
and in doing, by doing in righteousness, all
will come to you running over.
When doing in corrupt ways
no one can expect good, but only bad in every way.

Thought in *Spirit* being led by *Spirit*
is but thought that controls, being mind over matter,
but *doing* by one's own will, right or wrong,
man must know himself!

To express displeasure in another's action
is but expressing displeasure with one's self,
because of the fact of *choice*
of which the one choosing has complete control;
in which the factors of learning or behavior
takes precedence in
Leadership or Submission!

DADDY

Lester Joseph Steven Goode, born in Calhoun, Georgia;
raised in Saint Elmo, Tennessee, the quiet man, known
to many in Texas as *Slim*, had the blood of Cherokee
Indian Nation coursing through his veins.

The love of horses and being out of doors was the life for
him. So at the age of sixteen, he enlisted in the United
States Army. Fort Bliss, Texas would now be his home.

Looking for something that was known only to him led this elusive
man trying to find the place that was meant only for him. The
quiet place of peace, comfort, and pride that every man searches
for; the place that compares to the one held inside: Respect,
not admonition; Honor, not violence; Praise, not negativity.

People have a special place in their heart and mind
that opens only to a few, *a special few!*

A great man, a quiet man, sees this in many people. He
is accepted and invited into the special place of many, but
seen by very few! Although I write with shaky, unsteady
hand, the thoughts I project are about my Dad.
The man to me was kind and generous with what he had,
the love that he showed to his children was never ending.
He gave all that he had and left us with his *Pride!*

FLOYD '99

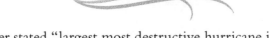

Newscaster stated "largest most destructive hurricane in size,"
the path was plotted and news was flashed.

Unknown citizens packed up and were ready to *move out fast.*
Two million plus flooded roadways,
the largest peacetime exodus *Ya ever did see.*"

As for me, *Well, I'll just sit back and ride it out*
This isn't the first hurricane for me, nor will it be the last.

I went to the river, *just to check out the tide.*
That's the way I know whether to stay or go.
The river was about normal.
Ya see, If a big wind was comin',
tide would be high and there would be water downtown.
Saw grass says that this won't be more than a bad nor-easter.

Skeptics say *You're a fool to stay.*
Ya know how peaceful it was after they all ran away?
The hounds were in their house well protected and dry
out in the backyard, still close by.

Well, Ole Floyd came on by,
and now is the time to clean up all of the debris;
the yard is full of leaves, the banana trees are ragged and torn.
There's no loss of livestock or life, so I guess you can say
it was just another windy day!

HURRICANE

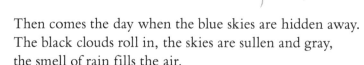

Then comes the day when the blue skies are hidden away.
The black clouds roll in, the skies are sullen and gray,
the smell of rain fills the air.
A strong *nor east* wind does prevail.

My dogs tell me *through their keen sense* that
strong weather is being heaven sent.

A lone Mocking Bird sings a cheerful song
while perched in a hardwood tree.
Chirps of a Wren comes from afar as the windblown rain descends,
others join in.

A big truck's engine whines
as sound comes from the east where the road follows the
San Sebastian River which flows with the tides.

In the past *oh, about the '50s,* when the hurricane would
come, the *storm surge water* filled the terrain. The river
would flood and water would fill every low
spot in *St. Augustine Town.*

You could not drive, the horses were kept safe,
water was knee deep, and you had to walk.
The only thing to do was just to *sit and wait.*
After all was said and done, the fishing was great
after the storm was gone!

FIELD

The vacant field needed something,
so a seed acquired from the sunflower
was planted in the needed vastness of green grass.
The heat from the sun, the water from the sky
caresses the pulp and one lone stem emerges.
Growth is assured, but stature is determined by the weather"
Not enough and the height will be small;
Too much and the seed will grow tall.
The lone seed is a start.
The vast array of flowers found in the yard today
is but a glimpse of things to come.
This, started from the lone seed planted
in the midst of vast green grass in the vacant field
that needed something.

THE FAST TRAIN

Writing the song of the fast goin' train
is the song of the freeman
traveling places that won't be seen again.

The lonesome sound of the steel wheels
saying *clickity-clack*, I ain't comin' back,
the sharp shrill of the engine whistle.

Travelling over hills, rivers, and lowland grades,
the song is always new.
Young 'uns wish to ride
to move on to the other side
where times are better and the going is easy.

So, get aboard, son, with your dreams in a bag.
The days grow short, time travels on this train won't stop,
slow down, or turn.

Ya better get on, *There's daylight to burn.*

FLORIDA PANTHER, NATIVE BLACK BEAR

The hunters laugh and talk of the hunts in the past, as young
boys and men would gather before dawn while waiting
for the first light so that fresh tracks could be found.

The secrets of life are seen and found by the outdoorsman.
The local heritage that a person is born with, whether
Spanish, Minorcan, Indian, Negro, instills a way of life that is
derived from hunting, fishing, living from the outdoors.

Never taking more than a person needs, always aware to leave enough
for another day, the *Ole Hog Bear* was what the Black Bear was called.

Where he lived was back in the *Guano*, north of St. Augustine. The
Oesterreicher, Leth, and Mickler families lived and hunted there.

The time started to change and people began to build homes
in Palm Valley, and this is when the Florida Panther started its
demise; not from hunting, as much as by cars. The cats, trying
to cross busy highways, would be hit by speeding cars, and thus
the story goes *About the Florida Panthers and the native Black Bear.*

BLACK HORSE JOE

Down in Florida, a story's told of a *wild* daring Indian breed called
Black Horse Joe
This man of mystic power and wonder lived deep in the swamp.
Story goes that he was born to be wild, *a breed apart*
from local civilized beings.
Ole Black Bear kept him alive. He ate, lived, hunted, and played with
the likes of the wild, and so he stayed there deep in the swamp.

He would always know when civilized man would
come. He watched close by, *never* to be seen.
Man would try to rule nature with money and stone,
until they found that this couldn't be done.
Here today, gone tomorrow.
Black Horse Joe's power never failed with *diligent* thought.
His ideas would prevail raising fish and crops galore for
people to enjoy, living with animals, not destroy.
For every planned community, condo, golf course
built, is thought given for natural wildlife?
For every creature destroyed today, mankind
will be affected later in the food chain.
Black Horse Joe
knows time and days when *civilized man*
will either change or fade away.

FALL TIME

Babbling flow of the waterfall, every swirl
of water as goldfish dart below,
with crickets chirping while gentle breezes
carry yellow butterflies away from
flower petals to a big bellowing fig tree.
A child goes playfully by, lost in their pleasant world of
dreams and thoughts gone by!
A blatant beauty of fall afternoon pictured in
the backyard setting of rural south
on a Sunday afternoon with a fire in an outside fireplace,
water tumbling over the rocks of the waterfall,
a distant sound, a drone coming from a blimp overhead,
the dazzling rays of sun passing through ghosts of wind,
calling children to let their handmade kites test the heights for
freedom in a vacant *sky!*
Time passes, fire needs tending.
Looking towards a new barn sits and ole lawnmower resting,
waiting to be put away.
Fire burns on, from sticks to embers, then to coals.
Oh, mercy me! exclaimed a flower to a bee,
I've grown so tall, my petals so large,
how will I find someone to gather enough pollen to regenerate me?
Look, here comes *Mr. Bumble Bee!*
The rain tree stands tall and gaunt, an ever
present century that overlooks
nature's abundance.
Tiny frogs travel through grass, eating; time
for all creatures to prepare for
oncoming winter and nature's plants to
conserve living parts to make ready for spring.

THE EVENING TIME

The night starts to descend.
This is the time when the whip-poor-
will and the crickets begin to sing.
The evening songs begin to chime,
voices of different creatures all the time.
The stars above shine with heavenly splendor,
in the grand concert for life's every gender.
The stars above shine with heavenly splendor,
in the grand concert for life's every gender.
Live passes by, the many sounds of creatures ebb.
The evening grows, nigh a time for all things to drive away to sleep.
The time for angels to whisper in quiet voices
telling of heavenly things and places to go and things to see.
The nightingale and tern, birds of flight,
together they feed, bathe, and frolic in the cool evening night,
passing the days heat in sheer delight.
A frog calls out for rain, another joins in,
the voice of many call out for rain.
The song rings out for all to hear,
life carries on in a distinct refrain
calling out asking for life-giving rain.
The mockingbird, the morning dove, blue jay,
and cardinal use the brown birdbath and fly lazily by.
A beam of moonlight outlines a lone dragonfly.
This is an evening for love and memories
to linger and to just not pass by
then in the mind to stay forever and a day.

MY DAUGHTER

One beautiful summer morn on the Matanzas riverbank
is where she was born; the child of beauty and grace
has encountered
but a portion of life that yet she will face.
The closeness I felt when she was small,
has not been taken away, *just hidden* is all.
These past nineteen years, each passing day,
has brought the bond of love closer to my daughter and me.
Growing up, the lessons learned are:
if you don't succeed the first time around,
just get up and start all over again.
When you are young, things seem hard.
The older and wiser you become, the easier they are.
So whenever someone tries to embarrass you to make you feel bad,
perhaps they are doing that
because they wish that they could possess
the things that *you* had.

CHICKENS

The ever so cunning and docile this beast
that is so beautiful to look at and *so* delicious to eat.
Clever young fowl are quick and fast scratching in the soil
for nourishment to eat.
Ah, at last a plump worm, what a feast!
Hurry, scurry, scratch, and seek, turn over the old twig
looking for a fat bug to eat.
Night time falls, time to roost, someplace above the ground,
high overhead, a safe place to be when Mr. Fox comes around.
When the moon goes down and a sun starts to break,
this is the time when the Rooster sings
Cockle doodle doo, good morning to you!

A COWBOY'S DAY

The morning sun peeks through the cypress branches, dew
laying heavy on the grass. Gingerly you load the horses
into the stock trailer for the trip deep into the low pasture.
The dogs are loaded and seem anxious to work.
At the top of the low pasture, just inside the gate, the horses and
dogs are together as a team. When the penning lane gates are opened
and the pasture gates are closed, the cowboys and the dogs depart.
Rounding up the cattle into a group, then moving them into
the lanes leading to the large catch pen requires patience,
timing, and skill. With a trained horse and dogs, all is
accomplished before noon. Dividing, separating, all is ready.
When the vet arrives, the toil begins with your hot shot, whip,
cane, or stick, all handled in a smooth, rhythmic tone: Roping,
branding, worming, and, *oh, yes,* placing a numbered tag in one ear.
At lunch, everyone piles into the trucks and goes to the *colonel's* for
a chicken lunch. Back at the catch pen, the toil resumes again.
Yearlings and un-bred cows are separated, for when Mr.
Sanchez arrives, they will be loaded and transported
to Gainesville town to sell at the market.
The sun is starting to get low, but the day is not complete.
Everything is loaded up and moved to the back pasture for
tomorrow's cattle penning will take place on *Tillman Ridge!*

CHRISTMAS

On a young December evening, sitting on the front porch swing,
the evening is young, a full moon is on the
rise, and the sky is a clear bluish-gray
with wisps of light, airy clouds are drifting lazily through the sky.
The sound of a hoot owl comes to the ear;
the sound after a while turns into the
A-Woo, A-Woo cooing of doves.
In the distance, a train's horn can be heard.
This alerts hounds and baying
begins and lasts until after the train has passed by.
The silence of night is soothing and warm.
The colors are calm for the night creatures.
The thoughts at Christmas time are supposed
to be gentle, warm, loving.
All of these things are enhanced with the
ancient smell of burning wood smoke
emanating from some distant fireplace
and flowing through the air in a cool fall breeze.
The rustling of leaves and shadows flowing across the lawn
lets the imagination become reality
and the morning returning to the original and sane!

THE CHANT

Oh, Great Creator, *Come to us during these troubled times,*
is the chant heard from the People of the Nations.
In the great circle of life, my blood comes from the Cherokee;
where I grew up was the land of the Seminole.
Today man has the power to fly like the eagle,
cunning of the fox, strength of the
bear, and wisdom of the owl.
The way that he uses these things are the way mankind shall go.
Is it not too far off that again we will see
the big herds of the great buffalo?
Is it not too late to again drink from clear
mountain streams without getting sick?
I have seen in other countries how industry pollutes the air,
when man, woman, or child cannot stand on
a hilltop, take in a long breath of
clear air, and say with a big smile *It is good to be alive!*

BLOWING WIND

On a blustery day on the outskirts of town,
a gust of wind blows the maple tree's branches down.
Among these, tucked safely away, are two newborn squirrels,
the nest safely constructed, warm and soft, yields two tiny babes
with bulging eyes, skin so bare, not even a hint of fuzzy hair.
It isn't long before mamma arrives, surveys the situation,
and checks for the babes' care.
In an instant, she reacts, picks up a babe in her mouth,
and disappears.
In a flash, she reappears as before,
and the same reaction she takes.
After securing the second babe,
she is gone as before.
Alas, this moment of truth is seldom seen by mortal man;
perhaps life's tales could be told,
if the human would only see what the
All Mighty provides for you and me!

BEACH FISHING

A Short Story by: Lester Goode

Sitting at the long oak table, eating raisin bran cereal
and milk, thinking of the time that Johnny Boy came
by the house and said, *"We're gonna all go fishing!"*
I hollered back, *"Okay!"*
He said, *"We need another truck."*
I got in my truck and followed Johnny down to the
restaurant. That's the place everyone would meet.
Big Johnny owned the seine net; Roy would run the surf boat.
Traveling to St. Augustine Beach, we went on just north of Butler
Beach State Park. At first, we traveled south towards Crescent Beach,
looking for fish. After traveling well past Crescent Beach, almost
to Fort Matanzas and the Inlet, the telltale signs of fish were not
seen. Returning down the beach to just north of where we started,
we pulled all of the trucks and boat up to the high water mark.
We would wait on the fish.
Chester and his crew were putting their boat in and setting their
seine, but to no avail. After taking a short nap, waiting for the
tide to change, Big Johnny said, *"That Delaney called and said a
big school of mullet passed the North Inlet and was moving south."*
We talked about setting that school of fish, so we agreed and
started traveling north. Chester was ahead of us, so we moved
slow. Chester decided to put his boat in the water. We passed their
crew after they set and retrieved their seine, no fish. Chester's crew
was reloading the seine net back into their boat as we passed.
There was a courtesy between fishermen on the beach: When fish
are located, one man's crew does not crowd the crew that located the
fish, just move on down the beach a few miles before setting your net.
Returning south to Versaggi Road, we stop, awaiting word of
the mullet school that had been traveling south. I walked over
to Big Johnny's truck to see what was going on. Big Johnny
and his daughter, Audra, were talking when I walked up.
I asked, *"Why are we sitting here?"*
They said, *"Waiting for the fish."*
I replied, *"The fish are here. If you don't set now, you'll miss 'em."*

Big Johnny has poor eyesight. That's why Audra goes
with him. Big Johnny tells Roy, *"We'll set the seine."*
The boat is dropped from the rear of the truck and re-
hooked to the front so it can be pushed into the surf.
Ed walks over to me and says, *"You ride the bow."*
A big person usually does that so the boat will not flip in the surf
and better control can be maintained. Roy and me jump into the
boat. Big Johnny pushes the boat into the surf until it floats, the
crew spin the boat around, heading it into the waves while pushing
it into deep water so that the outboard engine can be cranked.
After the firing, the engine and engaging the forward gear,
the boat leaps forward into the oncoming waves. The tether
line from the net is held on shore, the boat moves straight into
the ocean, and after clearing the outermost breakers, we turn
parallel to the beach, stretching out the net around the fish.
When all of the net is out, we turn toward the beach and ride
headlong, racing with the waves, running the boat fast and hard
up on the beach. Jumping out of the boat, the net line is handed
to one of the crew. This is when there is a truck at each end of
the net, they have special bumpers constructed for the front of
the truck so the net can be bundled up, a piece of rope wrapped
around the net and with a swift counter wrap locking the hold.
This is when the drive of the truck slowly backs up towards
the high water mark until the bag of the net comes ashore.
We set the net Friday afternoon. After pulling the net
closer to shore, Big Johnny yells, *"Stop and lock 'em down.
We'll wait until the tide falls so we won't bust the net!"*
There was so many fish that we had, be backed the
trucks into the water and started loading fish.
Ms. Audra and Big Johnny started calling buyers to sell the
fish to. People started to gather, beach police and marine
patrol. The point was made clear that we would have to clean
the beach. Nonstop we loaded and hauled fish all Friday
night, all day and night Saturday, and all day Sunday.
The beach was clean where we caught the fish. All Chester
could say was, *"I need somebody that can see the fish!"*

ADVENTURE OF TWO

Every moment of life is gratified with beauty and truth!
Seeking light is but to hear your voice.
All too often when talking with you
being intertwined through thought without common bond,
journey is all but naught only voice nary a touch!

Every moment of life is gratified with beauty and truth!
Adventure of life with you is like reaching a peak
when the world's hidden beauty is revealed
through your *smile* deep in depths of amber
colors forever in your eyes,
a Garden of Eden is seen!

Every moment of life is gracious with peace, love, and truth
in thee, I find the latter three.

The quiet demure of your being
hides many things that are revealed
only to me!

Thought of Time and Rhyme consists of original verse penned
relating to three different periods of life. In each period, you may
feel the attitude of change, not only in the person, but in the land.
Verses tell of that time, feelings of the day that are relevant for that
place and time, from a personal pint of view. A view of *DREAMS*.
Living through days in the life of this young Florida boy,
growing into adult, situations encountered and what happens to
ecology balance when humanity floods a serenity place, trying
to hold onto places and lands that have survived where they
were originally, over 437 years past, without radical change

TOLLING BELLS

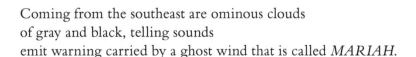

Coming from the southeast are ominous clouds
of gray and black, telling sounds
emit warning carried by a ghost wind that is called *MARIAH*.

Soundings carry striking deep rolling claps of
thunder, almost like bells of *NOTRE
DAME*, high into the heavens that soar to
tell of promise; some moisture may
come to replenish life in a parched land.

Often heard and scary of thoughts, sounds
of *being*, these times are rot with
individuals who worship the unknown for
reasoning of their own, only to cower
when *CLAPPING THUNDER SOUNDS*.

These bells of nature toll for nature's sake
alone, gift given to all to use or not,
nature's bell shall toll constantly.

Enjoy the *TOLLING BELLS*.

TIME

A consumption of which all adhere and partake of like in days of yore
when time was relevant with never-ending
days, nights filled with stars
in a heavenly blaze filling the sky as they do today.

Souls past return new again to follow the
same path in different stature;
ideas of the day considered new, alike, but advanced so they say.
Same as the first, made easier, faster, without delay.

Time most advanced is fable of today.
Wars as before, killing as before,
world advanced or returning to past as in days of yore?
When wealth was strong for but a few
and humble yet weak were ones they slew
for power to possess earthly treasures,
more you had is what made you great.
Learn from the past to keep a path straight.
Follow your dreams and you, too,
one day can possibly be great!

TODAY'S NEWS

Signs of times show a world to grow!
Only forecast *not to fail* in Today's News.
Human race is in disgrace with killing and wars,
beyond this I see a calmer, quieter door
someplace for *me!*

Today's News is a *constant* thing; if not *new*
just tell it over again, but in a different way, for
people to enlighten their hungry mind's eye.

Journalists clam a right to *write thoughts they
think correct*, then profess *not* to *discriminate*
or ruin human emotions and life.

Today's News is constant, you see.
Life, like thought, is new every day!

VICKY ... TO ME

Through thick and thin, as a constant friend,
always there to help or mend, my mistakes of verse and pen,
so humans may relate an ever profound beauty in mind and soul
is *Vicky*, a friend with spirit of *love* to share with worldly chores.

Life is filled with beauty and grace,
of which dance is thought to be greatest,
for students to learn this art,
which is bestowed upon *her* to teach.

Teaching this art belongs to few,
beauty of which is enjoyed by *all!*

Vicky lives this chosen path of beauty,
so fine in a time or place that is given.
Only to enhance, build for evermore,
when civil grace and beauty *is called for!*

WHO AM I?

Days go rapidly past,
thoughts in mind of linage arouse status woes;
fighting between *two* singles or infinity amounts create a line of
Who am I?

People, Cities, Nations claim to profess to be *right!*
Hostility still prevails in this world day and night.
Being biggest in strength doesn't mean wars will not be fought
and annihilation of people's race is not the road to take!

Seek to find a *true, honest person* has become passé
for legal and religious individuals in world society foray.
Where will humanity see and how can it be resolved with
truth, compassion, humility and stability for individuals
worldwide like *you and me?*

A good *man* is sought to lead today,
but will it take a good *woman* to show the path to take?

WORK'S DAILY "GRIND"

Words of a poet coming down
may find a lyrical note
in a daily grind of a city or town.
To this I say
"Poetry is Profound"
then toddle off to find a morning edition
of the regional *grind*!

Still others believe, so to speak,
it is to *grind* a morning's steeping brew of
coffee to drink.
Again, dancers sway with a *bump* and *grind*
to chase their feelings away.

Many say *to grind in mind* is to play thoughts of pain
that will not go away! Story forever of a *daily grind*
would be to say *I've done it before!*
I'll do it today!

TRUNDLE AND TROD

Trundle away to bed at night, perhaps trod across a lawn,
Earth moving at given speed as men trod on to their home.
A maiden trundles through golden flowers on the side of
Juniper Hill.
At evening time cows trod home to eat and give their milk.
A young man sits in frail sunlight composing lyrics to please
the young maiden, a song of which he sings to her as they both
Trundle down the mountainside in happy lyrical ease.

CHILD AT PLAY

Aloof, not castigated, fervently being a child at play,
romping all day in sunshine, playing in sand plenteous,
discovering actions newly learned, happiness always!

Mom is beginning to show things you will see day after day,
to grow and achieve starts with child's play!

Returning home with cheeks rosy pink, and a big healthy grin,
relates fun had on a beautiful summer's day, a day conserved for
children at play.

Tomorrow will be a treat, for this will be
the first kindergarten school day,
training a young mind, enhancing friendship in *child's play!*

Once growth to adulthood has been achieved,
reflections in mind tell of your life,
and how it all started and what you have accomplished,
starting with simple *child's play!*

FLOWING DREAMS

Inner ear depicts scenes only you can hear,
festooned with flowers cascading down a wall of
infamy of your life for all to view.

Reasoning wafts carelessly through stagnant
air in troubled times only to emerge
into heavenly pools of flowing blue water
scented by luscious vibrant honeysuckle
vines intertwined in different sweet-smelling roses.

Finding your way in a forest overgrown with
sanctions and hypocrisy instilled on man could surely lead
to decay of soul, thus finding mankind
awash in a sea of fraud and guilt.

Reasoning complexes all
when the foundation is not strong,
only ensuring that towering structures will one day fall.
When and where confuses us all.

HAPPENING

Senses prevail to deliver thought of which the path isn't new,
just lightly trod.
Past does again reflect civilizations before *lived to support humanity.*
Today action excels beyond the mind's comprehensions
into delicious levels of time!

A person's thoughts projected through *space*
lingers in a sphere circling in the
universe until a compatible void is found in humanity.

Dates and time are irrelevant, ideas vary, while
the basis of the same is a constant
structure of which changes shape: Cylindrical,
triangular, or oval to rectangular
remain the same, of these *ideas* begin!

COLOR OF EYES

A color of skin is not *who you are*, maybe *just where you've been*,
not *what* you are.
A common given is "color of eyes, black,
green, blue, or colors in between!"

Rules of today are not because of the color of your eyes
you are made to stay away.
Color of skin is rule of the day for others, unlike you, to keep away.
To never accept the lifestyles of least, or a blue-eyed
maiden cast adrift, and dark-eyed people who knew
that tune, helping this person her soul to regain.

Color of eyes, not seen in *bloody wars*, just
men of different-colored skin doing
battle, it seems, to right a wrong for Mankind
to decide *which path to travel*, in
life's never-ending trod!

HAPPY BALLOON

Fortune seekers throughout time look to contain *mass in mind!*
To entrap a spirit so they will be happy and content
through time often spoke of, never found
and ability for humanity with *love* all around
finding happiness day to day through sharing a piece of meat or bread
with another *never* wanting repayment again.

Balloons are gay to see *floating around light and free,*
Notorious humans of history try to expand on birds of flight in sky,
to find out what and why,
nature's animals are happy until they die.

Your life, like the balloon, when contained
floating happy and free there forever,
until its burst and *your mind is then set free!*

GIFT

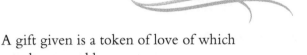

A gift given is a token of love of which
numbers untold cannot surpass.
When given with open heart, the gift is but a memory,
something that cannot be lost or taken away,
something that will last for eternity.

My personal gift is given to all, so that they may say a kind word
when I am no more.
Thoughts remain when mortal flesh is gone,
thoughts but seem to retain longer than pain,
thoughts of happy days when, as a child, you would play,
never a care, knowing *love* would always be there.

A gift is given in different ways, of which I deem uncertain
for me to say,
for as I speak, a gift will be given to whom?
I know not or why!
This gift that will be given by one to another
supposedly comes from *love*
of which there are connected thoughts
that will remain in the giver's heart.

A gift of love is given in numerous ways:
a simple smile or perhaps a wave,
the most gracious of these are a *smile* and *hello*!

DRAGONS OF ALFA

Deep in mountains of Southeast Asia, in
rice paddies of South Vietnam,
they prowl at night, gone when the morning
sun arrives, leaving not a trail
for others to find, only evidence left, pieces of flesh, on the ground.

Living on the side of a hill next to *Mira Flores Lock,*
dragons in South America like to take
stock of man, money, and drugs.
Of these, man and money, they hunt day and night!
Hunger of money starts a feeding frenzy of men.
This is when the dragon comes out, the only evidence left,
pieces of flesh, on the ground.

Dragons of Alfa are never seen, never known,
but alive, knowing *the job has been done!*

FLYING AWAY

Casting aspersions into a void, hoping space will absolve
wending waves, not penetrating sense of personal sounds,
dashing full against bastions in the mind, all too often tumbling
earthward, only to crash into unfathomably minute particles
of distrust. Sashaying into channels, wallowing in mire,
skimming across and through mind-streams found inside of
thought, portrayed in *dreams*, activated for reality's cause!

Drinking a *sacred* potion of *peyote root*, visions to come is looked
upon as access to a world not seen by humans before, traveled by
a *holy man* among men to view the future for all; selfless ambition
causes youth of today to dream sweet dreams about *flying away!*

DRUDGERY SCENE

War's disability gives cause for *repent*, days of nothing,
morns o're a small country home,
where mother resides after 94 years,
always offering a helping hand to children,
grandchildren, so on and so on ...
Day has come when son's daughter arrives
with man child in tow,
saying she has been *kicked out* and has no place to go.
So a place will be made for lost souls in need,
and the table will be full of morsels to eat,
then before bed, there is bread with honey or jam,
most of all, this person will learn,
it's time to stand up *on your own!*

DAYS GO BY

Present goes too swiftly by, when as a child, days would linger,
thinking that if I go to sleep, tomorrow will quickly come,
and then a new beautiful day,
just made for me to play in, would arrive.

Days of yore, as noted poet's pen, often misunderstood,
was then to say something happened *past yesterday*.

Oh, but in middle age, the clock of time cannot be stopped.
So, on we go, on the treadmill of earth,
Not To Stop, But Beat The Clock
in never-ending days!

A DAY SO FAIR

A day so fair is when you see an old childhood friend,
one that distance separates!
The sheer anticipation goes dancing gaily through your brain,
just a beautiful joy seeing them again,
is pictured brightly in your mind's inner eye.

Heart beating frantically with rapid sequential beats:
pounding, thumping, raising outwardly the
weathered skin of your timely chest,
while years of past do forward strain to display,
so that *back then* is as today,
instantly rolled through mind play,
never lost, just filed away!

ESSENCE OF LIFE

Crawling through doors or on the floor,
life ever-present there does abound
to cast its shadow on the ground,
once a child grows into a man.

Feelings, when babes you kiss goodnight
or hearing first utterance of sound,
knowing its meaning ... *just for you!*

Sensation of renown when
a partner for life enhances your fate,
together, twine into one,
male and female travel on.

Feelings you have, when beloved die,
or rapid beats of heart when she holds your hand,
sounds of your child's cry,
or happiness seen when looking into your wife's eyes!
Suddenly, realizing what pleasure you have in the *Essence Of Life!*

MEMORIAL DAY BLUES

Heartfelt soul cries of days gone by while *truth* rings out,
or so it seems, within a hallowed hall it gleams,
forever sounding *as if today is better than yesterday.*

Voices scream out, but few are heard,
a bugle wails out a lonesome sound
when a soldier, his head at last,
will lay down!

Forever remembered on each Memorial Day
are fallen heroes of battles past,
while giving their *all,*
never knowing who will be next to fall.

This day of a grieving-fest is celebration
for ones left alive,
I guess.

Hallowed halls stand *gaunt and tall*
to show this world *We Give Our All!*

LEAN ON ME!

Throughout my years, I search for a companion
who will share love that I contain just for her,
in everything I do and say.
Piecemeal pranksters prey upon someone they think is not their sort,
taking advantage to advance in *society court*
rapid steps over friends so dear,
never seeing a shed tear,
because of love, not distain,
wishing well for another is misunderstood for greed.
Happiness derived from peace within
stymies those that have not found peace at all.

FORE ACRES STROLL OF FOUR

Cascading down the face while waters abundantly flow,
humanity marvels at nature's show,
seeking to hold in mind forever,
plus one day,
stillness in life's likeness is carried away,
likeness shown around the world
to spirit-captured heaven in sight,
Alive, but nay!

Forward you plunge, into depths
straining comprehension and cognizance held within,
unlike multitude of vastness by others seen,
your focus is in far greater esteem
held, for its unwavering beam
alien to wit,
there does abound vexes, foes, stumbling blocks,
Ah, troubles galore?

Defending, defeating all,
worldly champions do astound
heaven's above earthly bound
quarry of one to find and protect,
Spirit, Peace, Love, Togetherness found,
one leisurely taking *Fore Acres Stroll of Four!*

DOUBLES

You have arrived with profound words
said in a profound way, in trying to display feelings,
in words that relay distinct sounds
that everyone relates to!

Doubles, you say,
are some profound words,
but in different ways,
same as before, different today,
tomorrow will unleash yet another way,
same but different,
another's thoughts depict doubles.

Doubles, you say, received with thought,
sent with love,
Doubles, you say?
Are a profound afterthought, same
only said in a different way!

MONEY TALK

Morning's glory of infernal rush
to bring about a final hush!
Brought to my mind in whispers before a morning's glory,
two fetch for one's appeasement,
so life can be lived minus roar of a sucker attached
to bodily limbs
detracting and extracting sacrificial articles
to appease
The Money God knowledge,
of which people are forewarned
and should contain the label saying:
Caution, Credit May Be Bad For Your Health,
when used in excessive ways.

Not knowing, is the claim of many,
while cunning of others to use the law
to enhance their wealth to portions unknown
relegates turmoil in ranks
trying to confuse facts that now have been seen.
Time revolves to beginning, accusers are now accused.
While the fox was asleep,
hounds arrived, now the chase is on.
Phrase used is:
It's The Economy, Stupid!

FACING TRUTH

Facts of life are outwardly the same,
in-between is foggy gray,
to trod this path, keen sense is required,
to not vanish below the mire.

At each step, fate descends upon the head of every mortal man,
through life, good transcends over bad,
lighting the way for humanity.

Without direction, children grow as seed is cast,
to replace the last, by you, former is known.
Is what you strive for mirrored or new?
Facing truth in life is hard, but controlled by only you.

Sitting, wishing, *if only*, seems adamant in this day
wanting help in finding your way,
facts are clear that in giving of yourself,
rewards will take place!
The first step must happen in travel
from indigent to wealth!

JULY 4, 2002

A windows night of birth and fright,
when citizens gather to shout and play,
sounds depict battles galore to end
and keep this nation's peace.
Holy ground where soldiers lay
aware of souls there encased for posterity.

Who will forget times of past
when men fought for liberty and peace,
believing that conflict to be the last!

Time passes through a needle's eye,
always repeating *what was done before.*

Islands of life abound like mold on walls of ancient caves
since eons of time that passed
through a needle's eye!

IN SEASONS PAST

As a child, I ran free, living loving outdoors, ya see.
Years pass slowly at first, then after 21, begin to race.
Fifty years aren't much to me, in others' eyes aged, *Oh Me!*

Fun things I did back then seem not as carefree.
Today people and things travel back
on the avenues in everyday faces.

From animal trails to modern roadways,
the road of life changes.

The *Gift of Love* on the roadway of life
causes ruts of which the origin runs deep
for all it seems.

BOY'S LOST DREAMS

As a lad without a place to play, I thought
in my mind of great places and
things that one day I might have at my beck and call.
Dreams, to me, came naturally at first, then
faltered one day when a strong
nor 'east wind carried them away.

A person's dreams are a private thing, beheld
by none but available to all.
Alas, you see, that when a dream is let go in
an arrogant fray, a big wind comes
along and just blows them away.

My childhood days were happy, sparked with
play, nights filled with dreams
and thoughts for better days!

FATHER ABOVE

Multitudes pray to spirit of man,
created in time, searching for relief from pain,
humanity starts to grow.
To this, added stress beyond control.
For certain mortals, a realm of understanding flows,
all others out of control!

Order in that day was for man to lead the way.
Joseph and Mary, whose babe was on the way
knew their son Jesus would be the *Messiah,*
dying on a cross to free mankind of *sin!*

After laying three days inside a tomb,
he would arise to be mortal again.
Forty days later, from earth he did arise
to live inside of *Heaven's Door.*

Every time you help something or someone poor,
you grow closer to entering
God's Heavenly Door!

BABIES

Babies are what I call Tiana's kitties three.
"Snuggles, Gussie, and Bryers" are names of kitties
that have allowed me time and trust,
forming a link between animal and human, you see?
These loving things are close to me,
often mistreated by uncaring hands,
kitty cats are part of nature's band,
placed here to be part of life, just like us,
Don't-cha see?

MELLOW MOOD

Mellow mood beckons light coming from
the radiant glow of embers showing beauty,
skipping over grass tips,
as moonbeams frolic through a cloche of darkness,
dancing over, through and across water spilling from a rim of
waterfall, immersing into a pool containing many creatures
showing and authority with croaking, splashing,
as melodious singing rings aloud,
enhanced by a small whippoorwill.
Ravens play and splash at the water's edge,
all offered *free*,
as I sit on a wooden bench
near a pool under a large orange tree!

FAMILY

Family, of present, is like a sea, always there, moving constantly,
adding here, subtracting there, only to appear again:
Elusive one day, passively sleeping the next,
with undercurrents moving to shuttle streams of thought and ideas,
used to emancipate mankind or create a state of worldly goods.
Love, shared by two, expands;
from original beginning, cannot be found!

MUSIC

Sensation to the body when transmitted through space,
thoughts gleaned from words, spoken in rhyme,
rapid or slow,
like shadows before music thrives!

Ohms are in the air, electrifying body motions,
feet move, hips sway,
lips sing, bodies gyrate,
while happy humans play.

Music, to me, is when a child is born healthy,
grows to be honest and true.
Then in return, provide and raise their children
to the same tune!

MEMORIES

Even thoughts of gentle days in a morning haze
brings forth music inside of me,
outwardly rolling across meadow and plain,
bouncing from steeple to shire,
then caught in a breeze, heaven sent,
to bring laughter and happiness all over the world.

Happy days of fun and play
bring children together in a foray
at kiddies school playground,
while still another darts into corners of the mind
when foreign footpaths lead into valleys
held by armies that could only be conquered by you.

A childhood dream is real, it seems.
Oh, but, alas, after years, the meaning seems to dwindle back,
lost to the ever-present newness of years
only to return when you are old and gray.

HELLO

Hello is what I say to you each morning, as I pray.
The sound of a greeting, simple though it is,
seems enough when *Greeting A Friend*.

Distant though we are, you're always beside me,
in my heart!
Closeness felt over distance is *true*.
Devotion to one bonded in perpetual bliss,
distant but together,
through love of *life, laughter, and happiness!*

HOUNDS OF MIND

Gathered together in spirit, hounds of thought do abound.
The hunt that precludes is forewarned and tough!
These hounds of mind are bred for this chase.
Across the ditch lies a narrow trail,
one taken by many who try to escape life's jail.
My hounds, *Alas* and *Alack*, will run you down and bring you back.

One that travels this newly trod trail believes
themselves to be the first.
Unknown to many, like hordes before this
trail, has been trundled time and
time again, each thinking they were first,
as long as there are mortals, *You*
won't be the last.

Hounds of mind, a special breed, they're in your mind to use
one day when trouble and stress start voicing dislike
to what is known to humans as *The Daily Grind,*
troubles before troubles past,
allowing these things to control your mind.
Bring out the dogs to chase away
these negative feelings of dismay.

Lord of Infamy, Lord of right,
teach and lead me through this fight.
Along to protect me, my dogs of mind,
Alas and *Alack,*
allowing a way for me to get *back.*

FEELINGS

Jumbled up, packed tight, stored to arise through thought,
Sensations in play with touch, feel, seeing.
Explosions of *Love*, lasting forever,
only to be killed by uncaring words or actions.

These magnificent explosions of feeling let senses of love generate,
only to be carried away by lust.
A truthful, honest man, who, like poetry in motion,
desires love! Not play that relegates man to be treated
as verses that can be added to or deleted!

How my mind rides waves of thought,
endlessly searching crannies, nooks,
vastness of earth, desiring to find the *love* of one true girl!

ST. JOHN

Way down south in a little Florida town
where I was born, inside the county
of St. Johns, a fortress city called St. Augustine stands built by men to
remain strong, still here today and viewed
constantly with admiration, not
disdain.

Custom of the day, to name cities for saints,
housing and shame none of
the same. Surly folk who's *god* was gold and goal was to conquer all
people and nations, yet unknown to instill rule for *God and King*.

These songs of lore with cords of string and rhyme
play on through time of malaise, cords strum in rhythm
as workers cast melodious sounds longingly
into medium of space, singing
to relax muscles that ache from constant working hard in fields
or on docks loading tonnage to sail away!

Rumors expound from lips unbound,
through vacant fields in mind to which rebounds
a given rhyme; given to many, heard by few.
The rhyme reasoning: *Love, Peace, Harmony!*

ONE BEING ONE

The Toll Road to Tranquility is no more for you or me.
Finding peace within oneself is like moss living on trunks of trees!

We are here, stated fact, to live or die;
to have or not, the goal is at the end.

Daily grind is at hand;
completing each will result in the latter.

Believe in yourself!
To be yourself is the hardest task of time.
Peace of mind,
the hardest thing to find.

One that knows who they are in time,
like standing raw milk,
to the top,
cream will rise!

SALT

Salt of time enhances a person's mind while gathering wedges that
constitute a mortal's soul, doing what you feel confident in to regulate
boredom or drudgery of days when riding
life's sea of unending waves.

Hurry, scurry, dance about time is money!
Or so they say.
But wisdom alone without actions doesn't produce results that you
anticipate.
Some believe as they know,
their best is their contribution to life.
Others that contribute believe their worth greater.
So the void is created.

Life's anchor in mankind is belief toward a goal,
which causes people to find a friend.
In doing this, a person fills their void of rapid decay.
Salt of life enhances meat when partaking
at the table of *society's meal!*

SEARCHING

Lighting a life of contentment sears into the rain,
searching for a woman to ease my mental pain,
constantly aware of *love* flashing instantly,
then disappearing as fast as it came.
Art of love is practiced by a female,
something given when needed, not a constant;
there when negative or positive actions are confronted.
A simple smile can be given in either way to arm or disarm feelings,
either positive or negative.
As ancient warriors searched for a dream,
so, too, do I dream of a love so true,
a love of a man for a woman, giving his all;
not just money, property, and such,
but *truth, honesty, and care.*
An honest man cannot play,
for the games of today are tainted.
Females treat a man's body, but cannot touch his inner soul;
a portion of which this man searches for,
someone to fill a void inside my inner soul
that can be filled by one that
shares my thoughts and innermost joys.
Thoughts continue to flow.
One holds the key to open the door of my heart;
where and when is a fact unknown;
the answer is found by turning the key
that will unlock this tender door, to find a constant love forevermore.

ODE OF PAT & MIKE

Journey today returns days when life was slow and easy,
chance provides later enhanced by time,
a child becomes a man when viewed through eyes of age,
time alone stands still.
Reverting thought stimulates waves of brain!
Oh, to think of being back there again,
pangs forgotten, growing pains,
only enhance life of today as stated before
"When I was a child, I thought as a child.
When I became a man, I put away childish things!"

OBSERVING YOUTH

In today's society, a child will grow
to be what the great spirit has in mind.
Once told was the story that to believe
you would never die and live forever
in mortal man's eyes
was by was taking a bride and becoming fruitful,
and thus you create another to take your place.
In doing this,
your son may take your space here on earth!
Same as the last,
Just like before!

POEMS

The evening mist rolls across salt marsh.
After morning's rush of fulfillment, there is still a void.
Often looked upon, but never touching a solid,
these things ripen with age,
never consumed, just thrown away.

Often noted in a poet's notebook,
then placed on parchment for never-ending life,
only to come forth on a given day
when found in a box of litter thrown away.

Words of man unseen drift through
time on a *golden stage.*
Whether untitled or titled,
are words of *shame*
wafting there for times untold,
drifting away as clouds in the sky,
only to return, when *anger* arrives.
These words of truth by me may seem,
beheld by ones that *can only dream.*

MY SONG

My ears ring with joyous sound unheard by many!
One started at birth, sounding louder as I grow,
sounds of *life* for me alone, but clear, alive,
full of a song that I sing made just for me,
hidden away deep into a dark den,
now coming to light for all to see!

On with this song that only I can hear,
guiding me through this destiny of life!
Sounds are sometimes sharp; at other times mellow,
a sound so divine only a righteous soul will tend to follow.

When sounds are sharp, a solid stone breaks
as if shooting stars through a heavenly maze
cast wildly about with a plunk of heart strings
evenly strummed by nature's harp.

Tune of wildflowers throughout the countryside
over meadows, brooks so clear and fair;
never to disturb a sleeping baby deer up and over
hills and dales, across mountain peaks at headlong speeds,
over oceans and seas with minimum breath,
only to reform into great tempests along with death,
destruction, and mayhem on the way.

Alas, the torrent has passed.
Left in its place is Life, same as the last!

SUNDAY AFTERNOON STROLL

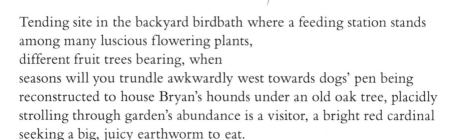

Tending site in the backyard birdbath where a feeding station stands
among many luscious flowering plants,
different fruit trees bearing, when
seasons will you trundle awkwardly west towards dogs' pen being
reconstructed to house Bryan's hounds under an old oak tree, placidly
strolling through garden's abundance is a visitor, a bright red cardinal
seeking a big, juicy earthworm to eat.

Next to rustic bard lays a quiet pool containing
goldfish that freely swim,
collecting morsels to eat. Frogs abound in
nature's realm, confined in this
Garden of Peace.

Traveling east, you climb a small hill upon
which stands a fruiting fig tree
closely surrounded by loquat trees under
which beautiful flowers grow.
As you saunter up the white stone path, you
pass grape vines growing their
new fall crop. Continuing on, a date palm is centermost found; a step
beyond stands roses with honeysuckle galore, sights, scents, pleasure
abound in my garden's afternoon stroll.

TEACHER CALL

Ms. Who, from Tiny Mites School has called to say
That Sickness has come to one so dear
and movement of nature is liquid run
for someone concerned should rapidly come
fetch away one so near,
so a diaper change can be done by *Mommy Dear!*

Alas and alack, rush of many to aid child,
but a mother's love is best of all!
Act of caring is portrayed today only to collect money paid.
When all is said and done, caring teachers,
make learning fun.
So to ones who fear the truth be told,
in feelings of grit
I write these words of whit
for people all next time you receive a *Teacher Call!*

AMERICA

The Negro, Jew, Irish, Chinese, the female,
children, and other minorities
all cry out and want to be heard.
The original, the first American Indian say little and still survives.
The latter is the one most overcome by all of the former.
The last shall be the first and the first shall
be the last to occupy and belong
to this land we hold fast.
Food aplenty and fortunes galore are two of the many things
that people search for.
Freedom for people from foreign shores is no more or less.
The land they departed is getting too crowded, I guess!

BONITA DE CUBA

Close, not far away, is this island of beauty
where people have hearts that
forever care in safety and love for people who were born there.
Warm winds send gentle breezes across Matanzas Bay.
Below Havana stands the small village City
of Lights, first to be burned
when pirates would attack.
This was told to me by my friend Jorge.
Georgette (Jorgetta) loved long
quiet walks along the shore with her dogs and friends by her side.
We, like two ships at sea, occasionally meet
in some place, port, or time.
Two lovers that live life as it is, but love
each other each time they meet,
as if it were the first time for each.

CHARACTER

A person is born and all is beauty and love.
As a child grows in mind and stature, things begin to change.
Two children as babes touch, play, and eat together.
When adolescents, they begin to grow apart.
The skin color is not the same,
so they are held apart.
The love and beauty they knew as a child
is dashed and broken into as many pieces as there are stars in the sky.
The only question asked is "Why?"

LISTENING

Art of listening is long and hard to learn.
It isn't derived from the inner ear.
An ear is used to hear.
Listening is from inside.
Have you ever been alone? I mean, really alone?
With just you and nature, at first you hear
and your mind registers, but do
you listen?
When you listen, you hear your inner self
speaking loud and clear the inner
person that guides and directs you!
When you listen, you can accomplish any
task, ones that are never hard but
are enjoyable to do.
This is done by listening.
You listening to *you!*

LOVE IS A BEAUTIFUL THING

Today I planted flowers,
always comprehending the ultimate beauty.
The temptations of my mind aglow
as the black hard embers of smoldering coal
just before they burst into the ever-burning
flames of fire.
The fire of love is like the hottest burning firestorm,
Consuming everything in its path.

LOVE

Even the sound of your voice
acts as a catalyst between filling the basket
of love or loneliness.

I always think, but cannot feel,
express, but not taste
the reverence of your smile.

Tender full lips, hair like an angel
in Picasso paintings.

A look coming from the deepest part of your inner soul,
through deep brown aster,
the color of your eyes!

Does a Garden of Eden
await the twain?

Making way through spaces of time.

ME

The road of my life is diversified and goes in many directions.
I love to create and accomplish tasks that are not every day,
but somewhat colored; not just humdrum, but alive!

To sit and enjoy sounds and colors, a realm
of tones coming from different
species of birds, actions of squirrels in different seasons.
Turning of colors when nature's foliage prepares for season's change,
cycle of life derived from contemplating nature's own flowers,
trees, birds, wildlife, and humanity!

Life is but a circle of the wheel!
Your heritage is guaranteed with birth of a child in the spring,
as if to say the spinning wheel contains all flowers,
trees, birds, wildlife,
and, look, *You Made Me!*

SPIRIT WOMAN

The Spirit Woman come from Jamaica Town.
Flowing black hair, bright sparkling dark eyes
and skin so soft and brown.
She smell so sweet
like petals from a flower that is heaven sent.

The flow of her body when she move
is as quick and light as the morning mist.
When she dance, the air is light.
She flows and glides as if the sun,
stars, and moon are by her side.

The Spirit Woman is the one to see
for the love potion that will conjure up
the one you seek.

SPLIT IN FLORIDA'S LIBERTY TREE

In year 2000, a new millennium ya see,
elephant and mule were racing with glee.
Race was run with honesty and truth flying free,
supposedly ones to benefit are you and me!
As the race was started, elephant broke free,
striding ahead, running calmly.
In the stands, everyone said *this race is over, elephant has won!*
Owner of the mule stated *it just started, it ain't over yet!*
Down south, Miami way,
elephant thought he won,
but bets were counted and it went the other way!
With a memory that *never forgets,*
bets were challenged and finish was circumspect,
day after day, all angles were tried,
elephant fans ranted and raved, then cried foul!
The four-legged beast just lowered his head
and calmly grazed on pasture grass.
At this point, people see that an elephant and mule
when running a race with *Good Ole Boys,*
the handlers down South where blood is thicker than water
and anything goes, to win a race!
Don't collect any respect until the race is complete!

THANK YOU!

For eternal dreams
For unselfish giving
For your ever-caring smile
For your glowing presence
For your unlimited knowledge
For your inner/outward beauty
For your unerring strength
For your ability to *Listen*
For placing others first
For *You* being *You!*

THE OVERTURE

The concert of everyday life sing a song of
ever-growing virtue. The beat
can be fast or slow.
The movement is constant, feeling the unseen
sound, the harmony flowing
endlessly through unending waves traveling rapidly throughout one's
mortal body.
The sensation entering the brain giving
eminent satisfaction and peace.
The daily work routine forms a constant tone, building into a grand
concerto stemming into finality.
The base drum sounds this is the tone set for all of the instruments to
follow. When the whistles toot and all of
the brass begins to sound, the
drums can be heard leading all with their deep, mellow sound.
The natural voice is the sweetest heard
and sounds so beautiful when it
utters calm, thankful words.
Words seldom used today, are the two, *please* and *thank you.*

TOUCH

In touching you,
a grasp of fingers intertwined while holding hands,
ease of movement and thought
while you allow my being to enter your mind,
not without care or truth, love or commitment,
but with an everlasting bond!

WRITING TRUTH

In weaving words of wisdom swell,
like throwing the cat into the well,
once at the bottom in water or fray,
oft times, there a person will stay!

The way out is slimy and tough.
You climb and strain,
but it is not enough.
Top can be seen to exit the trap.
You must seek the right path to follow
or you'll never get out!

TRIALS AND TRIBULATIONS

Skirting around issues,
sliding past acts,
everyday scene
politicians tend to regret.

Me, I muse about the fact
that bending a legal rod with
money isn't a magic trick.
Simply fact!

YOUR GOAL

A calming sense of reality is pounded into
your mind as each drop of rain
on a tin roof top. Years of life, hard as they
were, glide so easily through
your mind. Dreams of better things always hang there.
Precariously they dangle in front of your
mind's eye. They are there for the
taking as apples, oranges, pears are harvested, so too are your dreams
made reality! To believe is to do thus.

One's life is to progress for you. Solitude
of life, its problems and stress,
bring out unseen talents in a person.
Others try, but never seem to reach their
mark. More or less! More the
better, less the harder, you try to reach the peak of the *Mountain of
Success.*
Every person tries to conquer in their mind
and in their inner eye to reach
for that goal, each human seeks but never seems to find,
for they never really try.

TURPENTINE MAN

Traveling through dim-lit morning mist
to find, cut, and mark tall pine
trees, a long swamp trail only reveals sign
of wagon wheels and mule tracks
meandering slowly from tree to tree where cat faces emit sap that runs
through human-carved channels to give
direction so young golden resin
will flow into orange-colored fire-cast clay
cups once placed at the base of
a tree to collect and hold abundance emitted from the tree.
Retrieving its bounty, you glide silently across and through a green
palmetto maze!
The mule, with his ever-keen senses, travels
knowingly through dark black
foreboding swamp's haze returning home
to turpentine still, ever so alone,
nestled beneath large oak trees out on the ridge.
Big oaken barrels full of pin sap sit idly in
long rows where gray squirrels
have busily stashed acorns awaiting oncoming winter.
Dragonflies, with other flying insects, are
suspended in liquid, caught, held
in time, motionless and lifeless.
A woods rat scurries from between barrels.
Florida pinewoods is home for the Turpentine Man!

ON THE SHORE

Together we walked hand in hand along
the sandy shore, never a care in
mind in this place and time.
I always dreamed one day she would be
mine to live and love with our
passions combined!
Oh, but fate was nasty to me, for Suz, the
love of my life, didn't know me!
Paths of two star-crossed, it seems, would
meet forever and a day to be
one for life, most keenly aware, accepting
each for who they are and not
what they have done before!
Walking on water is not a feat. Knowing
who you are is toughest of all,
living and dying just comes in between.
Trying to be what others say is a
fluid motion, not a shooting star!
My senses become aware when you are near.
My life is fulfilled when you
hold my hand.
Love of one for one someday will be a never-
ending story for *Suz and Me,*
while we trundle along a vacant shore.

ONE SPRING MORN

Sitting under a tall cedar tree on a warm
Spring Morn, out of the corner of
my eye, I catch movement of a gray squirrel scurrying down a tree.
At the bottom, it pauses, its tail rapidly
flicking, while it tastes the air with
its nose.
After assurance, it hops through the chain
link fence and begins to search
the lawn for delightful treats.
A small reddish wren flies to the tree. Out
of the loquat tree steps a red
cardinal. Two mocking birds sing melodious
verses, as if to say, *Where are*
you? Where are you? From the power line another bird answers *Here am*
I! Here am I! But I am moving away!
From the old dog pen, comes chirping and
tweedier of small birds, gray and
white, sashaying and screeching in and out
of neighbor's plum trees during
a bird food fight!
Oh, yes, what a treat to sit under a tall cedar
tree on a Warm Spring Morn
to enjoy natures delightful show!

NIGHTLY HUNT

Flowing scented night air thought of pure
clear dawn, morn will arise with
sullen bold grace.
Even as though a just born creature gasps
its first breath, instilling glorious
life!
Feeling is, bond and same, passing on life's
road, one longs to see what one
passing has tread so lightly upon. Never
asking when or why, simply doing,
always searching for unseen goals, trying
to be celebrity with glory, glitz,
and praise: To be first! Always to be first!
People always love a winner!
Why cannot the multitude of society's conscious elite accept profound
happiness in the simple actions of life?

SEA OF TIME

Seas are here, seas are alive of which one comes to find something.
Is it the vastness or scent, maybe the sound that enters a cavern in a
person's mind, then explodes into realms
unknown, leaving articles aged
through time.
In wandering this sea of time and things,
does mankind change or just do
the same thing, but in different ways?
Thoughts of many, expressed in different ways, lead to a goal; same
thoughts, but interpreted in different ways.
Time passes. Ideas change from what to when,
and then start all over again.
Things never change, just built, torn down, then rebuilt again.
What is not here today will be there new one day,
just for you!

GARDEN

Planting of which sallies forth ever luscious
edible morsels of delight when
consumed nourishes body of humanity. Food from the earth made for
sustaining life need be replaced, now and then, to help the constant
growth of humans!

A vacant plot of land used to help man,
feeding one or many, by planting,
growing, harvesting simple rows of corn,
veggies, beans, thought, albeit,
taxing to do?
Pleasure derived from eating food that you
have grown is greatest of all!

Mankind will learn, never too late, food of thought provides body
nourishment naught!
Body growth, by consuming food, a daily source to humanity.
Where will food be coming from if man destroys and doesn't replant?

MONTANA MOUNTAIN HOME

Living in a mountain meadow with lush
grass for grazing, fresh mountain
spring streams bubbling clear, running fresh
over gleaming rocks on gravel
stone, deer, with elk galore, playful otters
constructing homes in this rural
Montana mountain Vail.
To this, I wish to live and raise horses where
only stars encased in the clear
night sky reflects a beauty made by God.
Non-human hands sculpt and carve to leave
their mark in a most wondrous
way for mankind to cherish and appreciate.
Wonder of one's inner mind depicts things
derived from nature's scheme.

MOUNTAIN MELODY

Even swirl of nightly growing sorrel stir
song sparrows bringing forth
melodious sortie of singing creatures emerging
upon northeast hillside of runner's hollow.
About this time, drifting across a wistful breeze
is a mournful happy religious tune,
sounds made holy by handmade fiddle, banjo, and do-brow,
sung with music straight from the soul,
tune humanity makes.
Twas a night of one that will never be again,
sound made from a newly born child ringing across hills
from mountainside and over glades,
a magic tone, *life anew,*
gathered into,
filed away,
and placed around a father's heart,
never to be torn away.

A DROP OF RAIN

Bright, radiant beams of morning *burst*
through open portals in a calm blue
sky. Mortals scurry, hurry beneath this all, never retrieving moments
casually cast away to be lost in time in
humanity's race for ultimate grace
and space.
Time sees a child grow as seasons change,
winds blow the earth into constant flutter
through vast expanse of clutter.
Flashing of colors on a mountainside,
water flushing from heights above slide down, around,
and frolic over through caverns of nature,
sculpting, carving, forming, doing.
Always doing.
A speck of dust gathered from desert so dry,
after hours wandering through a sullen sky,
gathering moisture beads, it grows so heavy,
and falls to earth, bringing life to nature's own
to be one again,
from whence it came!

BLACK CREEK

In a gumbo mud swamp where a black water creek flows
stands a rundown shack that only I know,
where black bear eat, deer, possum, and coon play.
Skeeters galore, frogs, snakes and the like,
live and abound without much sunlight.
Black Creek sickness took the family away.
Now people come to hear tales about yesterday
when the shack was a home for a family, you see;
now just memories, for but a few,
or tales to entertain folks like you or me!

CUTTING THE GRASS — IN THE SOUTH

August brings changes in weather, mosquitoes, frogs 'n things.
In gardens, nothing else much moving, except watching grass grow.
Mandatory cuts every other week requires stamina galore and a pure
hatred of dollar weed that seems to grow
everywhere you wish to cultivate
rare hybrid roses in.
Seemingly, grass planted on vacant hill has sprouted, sprang forth, and
needs to be manicured or threatens to
grow tall, obscuring scenery all!
Trudging barn-ward where John Deere is
kept, one clear afternoon need
share time required for mowing the hill: top, bottom, all around.
Homes where husband *honey-do* lives, keeps most current,
hottest machine on the market today,
for manual labor isn't his way, going out in heat of day,
mowing grass has to be done in fastest, easiest way
allowing fee time to kick back and watch football's *play of the day!*

DOGS OF MIND

Finding what there is to do, reasoning whole day through,
unabashed heartache before, history behind, deep running water
crossing in streams of life ahead, one of
multitude, to arise on evening trek
along footpath in mountain strain or tropical
forest much the same always
getting up after falling down.
Rehearsing to remember lines of thought so you can find a way back
when your mind is lost!
Hills and dales in nursery rhymes depict journeys thereof
to which a child is drawn when, as adults, they will go to explore,
look to find a truth found lying there
undisturbed by human hands from before.

OYSTERS LAY IN BAY

On this bed of gray covered by water twice today,
they're living, growing, continually harvested fresh,
placed on coals of golden-embered fire,
which opens a tightly closed shell
revealing luscious morsels to eat!
With nimble fingers, you scoop out oyster inside,
pop it into our mouth and slurp it down!
Oh, to taste this feast!

PENGUINS

Dreams to me are so clear with wonderful,
beautiful creatures of nature walking,
sliding on ice, white and clean,
awkward to us, so it seems.
In water, their movements are poetically just!
Movements so fluid, forms so free,
faces are happy, smiling with glee.
If life only gave these things
to you or me!

For Tiana, My Friend.

THOUGHTS IN THE WIND

As a stranded voyager stands stranded on a lost shore, he casts a bottle containing a note asking to be saved.

For me, I try to be as the one who stands alone and casts his lonely thoughts into the air.

Someone alone on a distant shore will hear my call and rescue me.

Play on night's wind and dreams during
the day help me gravely trundle
throughout dreary days.

My spirit is searching for its soul mate,
asking every note on whisks in the breeze,
carried on the songs that birds sing in trees.

Days go by here in thoughts so grand when
one day my true love will come
to me!

Beauty so deep, thoughts so grand will be the dowry my wife will command.

Love forever, her natural stand will be;
Love for one and only me.

ROVERS TIME

There just isn't enough time! Common phrase used by many.
Question is *Why Not?*
Too much pressure, I guess.
Wouldn't it be lovely to live without distress?
Weight of a world causes a beautiful body to stress.
Everlasting laughter helps relieve this often,
too common, press.
Laughter in amber eyes, show humility,
love to lighten days, tender, gentle touch that relights
smoldering coals of love erupting into raging wildfire,
skipping effortlessly across and through deepest canyons
unfounded places, darkest corners of a heart
illuminating everything, exposing all, not in shame, but delight!
Freedom to experience your thoughts with someone that you love.
Live life the way you feel at ease to do things
at your own pace and time!
Two people traveling in the same direction on the same road, *together*
entering life's mainstream, swimming together side by side,
always side by side.

THE SMALL BLACK BEAR

The small black bear journeyed into Live Oak town.
The day was nice, just right for a look around.
Things went well, you might even say fine.
After his afternoon snack, he looked around for a place to nap.
Things were crowded, people all busy as a bee,
Then, there it was, a tall pine tree.
Feeling tired and scared, he climbed to the top.
The people below stared and gawked.
The small black bear could not understand people talk.
Time passed on, the decision was made,
just leave him alone.
By doing this,
the small black bear will come down
and journey back home.

CHICKENS

The ever so cunning and docile this beast
that is so beautiful to look at and so delicious to eat.
Clever young fowl are quick and fast scratching in the soil
for nourishment to eat.
Ah, at last a plump worm, what a feast!
Hurry, scurry, scratch, and seek, turn over the old twig
looking for a fat bug to eat.
Night time falls, time to roost, someplace above the ground,
high overhead, a safe place to be when Mr. Fox comes around.
When the moon goes down and a sun starts to break,
this is the time when the Rooster sings
Cockle doodle doo, good morning to you!

PUP CALLED RED

Leaving security of tarpaulin-covered boxes,
Hound-pup scampers into the grass-covered yard
trying desperately to control four big paws.
Finding temporal delight in seizing and tugging
on grass or sticks with all of its instincts
and strength.
Not getting attention, pup attacks my passing pang leg,
as I slowly move past, falling, bouncing, growling, never letting go!
Kneeling down, filling a food dish, inviting
the inquisitive pup to stand,
with paws touching my ribs,
instantly with a *boom,*
falls flat on its back!
With a chuckle I say *Way to go, Red!*
Baby things are fun to watch and enjoy,
life is but an instant.
Learn to appreciate moments that are
awarded to you when they arrive.

RED PUP

They came one cold and dark night; skinny
and scared. With haste of movement,
warm food was prepared. One pup lasted
the eve, strong will kept him fed.
Next morn, he was spry as a newborn fawn,
alert, ever keen to things of life:
Barking and growling, as pups oft times do.
Alert to sound, so I called him Red.
This pup day after day grows and acts like a
prize pant-let chewer, following me
around, cries like a *sooner*. I laugh at his play,
knowing of his wealth that will
affect a *Good Dog* one day!
Hunters come from miles around to see the
likes of a first-class champion hound.
Worldwide tradition knows of action between *Man and his Dog!*

THE OLD BACK DOOR

Nestled there curled up on a rug, head between its paws, lays Red.
Not yet grown, just a making of a dog, this pup has made a bed.
When coming in there, he is guarding the kitchen door.
He is most protective of a bowl holding his food.
This pup, alert to be aware of all,
listening for his name to be called to run, sniff, play,
trying to make a *Good Dog* one day!

MY HOUND FRIEND

When planting flowers in a garden or pulling
weeds, the constant friend is
always there. Few have the pleasure of feeling the sensation when
kneeling beside an overgrown bed of flowers
pulling weeds to feel a cold
nose and fuzzy head nuzzle up under your arm.
As you pull that malingering ragweed, a
moist tongue laps your fingers,
then attacks the fern you just planted.
Starting to dig holes is funny, dirty
flying through hind legs, and then longing
look as if to ask *Deep enough?*

THE OLD HOUSE

An old house is weather-beaten and raw,
but still stands strong and tall.
Within its walls, secrets are contained that
only times long past can recall.
A ghost of moons long past still roams the halls.
Laughter and joy of children is gone.
Memories of generations past fill a vacuum of time and space.
People of today think life is but a game to play.
Some move fast, others yet slow.
The journey is hard and long, you say.
Some will succeed and others will fall.
This game of life is made for us all,
like the old house, weather-beaten and raw,
but still standing, strong and tall.

THE RANCH

Nestled deep in a secluded area of mind
entering thoughts that arise in periods of independence.
Days of hope breaking free from confinement
instilled through necessity!
Serene, quiet, natural, being one with nature,
not to destroy, but to let nature remain dominant.
Living in today's world to conserve,
never forgetting *Nature* is a loving child of *Mother Earth*.

COPPER

My ole glass-eyed, bald face Palomino
Horse came out of New Mexico.
The Spanish-bred cow pony knew more
about working cattle than some of
today's cowboys.
The horse is the soul of a lone person that only finds peace when he is
working cows, riding fence, or living close to nature.
The outdoors draws, calls, and offers freedom.
Having a true friend, companion and partner
is found in your cow pony
roping horse.
The saddest day was when I rode out to the
low pasture and could not see
the golden-coated horse feeding with the cattle.
Two days later, he was found down by the
water of the pond. He went to
get a drink, and he died.

HOUND DOG

The neighbor's hound dog has puppies,
some brown, some black as can be,
with long floppy ears and agility of all baby things,
and ever-present idea to investigate all;
to sniff, paw, bite or gnaw, the pups are a funny bunch.
Backyard cats are another story.
Sleeping in outdoor furniture,
walking through the yard with me,
weaving in and out of my legs as I walk,
causing me to almost fall down
trying not to step on their tails!
The days go by swiftly.

BUTTERFLY

With rapid, majestic movement,
the creature glides away.
The most delicate of animals,
the butterfly creates some of life's exciting moments.
The time you spend watching is but a moment,
a moment that will live in your mind.

BRIGHTNESS/BEAMS

Flavor of the sun cast forth.
Is it strawberry/orange,
lemon/vanilla?
Rays bursting forth are like sprinkles
of which
all are consumed
without thinking of tomorrow!

THE NATURAL

Laying where you are born, living in a
village where home is at hand for
more than 50-odd years. Sense of fellows born of same brings routine
instilled from past, hence the attitude towards
others when their ideas are
put forward.
Calm, laidback lifestyles now are threatened
by influx of civilization, loss of
natural resources that were controlled so
humanity would receive benefit
while conserving nature's wild beasts.
Now rapid growth claims lands of animals that cannot live inside of
manmade environments without hazard of being killed.
Offset feelings run rampant during public voting rage: Name-calling,
accusations, political vengeance instilled
on citizens today, as past, to be
elected to public office.
Murder and mayhem still exist within.
Doesn't anything change?

WOODED TRAIL

Within dense habitation of forest's realm
lives creatures in earthly domain
of mind seeking but time. Time that is oh,
so fine, brandishing through
forest walls engulfed in foliage differently
colored in greens and ambers,
shading, shedding, covering this trail leading
to paths so fragrantly moist in
morning's dew.
Path that leads to riches so bold, riches for life's being to be surely kept
well, magic moments with beings of power
controlling mountain spirits
who lead the way.
Thoughts in mind carry souls forward
over, around, through hardships
beset on mortal men. Trail leads upward through clouds misty with
dreams untold, releasing them to ones with
power. Contained in visions
given in spirit's holy juice, they drink to enter holy space.
After trekking along on this path to a holy
place atop mountain height into
sky closer to Great Spirit's home where man prays for peace of mind,
length of days, traveling on this wooded
path alone into forest's domain.
Traveling this track to reach a holy realm to find treasure of gods!
After doing so, what then?

WORLD OF WONDERS

Seems that every morn emits a different
remembrance, not just like day
before, always a bit different in some way.
Today I talked with an old friend, a person
that attended the same school
and was friends to everyone. Even if your
name wasn't known, Bobby's
name was!
Today, perhaps, in some way, I will pass
on to some unsuspecting person
a thought of humble love that will be passed on the same way,
without need or care, just done in your natural way,
without flash or flair,
to carry forth a dream once held for but a few
adding to life with loving care!

WALKING A DUSTY TRAIL

Found parted, not forgotten, lives of two enchanted spirits fling;
entwining emotions throughout universal realm.
Reflecting glow of seasons away
pass in gleam constrained within memory's bank!
Reliving sensuous moments while walking in moonlight's beam
holding hands and embracing spirits tightly!
Feelings of one delivered in faith
to another whose aura gleams
is not a sure case of love it seems?
Compassion for creatures, faith in man,
trying to be all that you can
describes a most stringent plan for life,
one unattainable by numbers of humanity!
Walking along this dusty trail of life,
often trodden by heavy souls embracing burdens
given with malice,
or less, performing grievous acts upon men of faith.
Again, faith beheld is not faith untold.
For humanity to carry forth, humanity must regain faith
in themselves once and for all!

ANIMAL EXCURSION

While roaming free, back woods trails
created by animals, the four-footed
kind, in this world are same as past, only change is time.
Food once plentiful now is sparse, creating new... why?
Crating massive structures ... for?
What, when, why?
When you die, things built will be torn down
for someone else to do their thing!
Animal trails still exist, these creatures once massive,
but smaller now, are still traveling these same trails.
Food, to me, is the reason why!

CANE POLE FISHING

Cane pole fishing is best for me.
Under an old cypress tree
my ole dog sits waiting for me
to catch big *Ole Bubba* catfish.
Daylight hours is not for cat fishing.
Best time had is just before dark.
Along a stream, you move to set bush hooks
that tell you when fish take a bite.
Ya set around a fire until moon comes up.
Ya check the fish line all through night.
Good hot coffee around a fire is part of the delight.
Waiting for *Ole Bubba* to bite.

DEAD HOG FOUND

Story is told of a *ranger* bold
hired for mercenary work down Florida way.
Job was classified tops for pay, anyone asking.
Joe was an eager ex-sniper looking to fulfill
his duty for God and The Man.
So he loaded his vehicle, headed south, to
do the job at Palencia to rid this
place of the dreaded wild armor-covered armadillo.
In choosing the correct weapon to use,
he would settle on the most vicious, ruthless, powerful gun,
the dreaded caliber of .22.
Day would come when the groundskeeper found a gun-shot hog
dead under a walkway bridge.
Truth is told that this man hired to kill,
while stalking ever-vigilant, armadillo prey,
took out pent up emotions on this wild hog one day!
Ending this story so bold is simply to say,
a person shooting animals for pay
needs to collect carcasses, clean up area,
or be on their way!

A FORAGE TRIP

Crisp, cool, an autumn morn beckons.
Peace, calm beauty of a national forest near Ocala holds history,
plus unbounded acres of freedom to roam.
This is where Jennifer and Bryan will spend this day,
quality time, time to find and understand,
learn from and about nature and life.
Locating a place to fish was found to be not as important as collecting
pine cones, grape vines, et cetera,
of which beautiful holiday wreaths will be constructed.
A most wonderful gift is the one that is
made by the person giving, as if to
say *take a small part of me.*
A part of one's soul will remain as a token
given with love and humility.
When overshadowed by a person's greed,
or dishonesty,
person giving will become more.
The ungrateful one will receive what they deserve.
Sun shines the same for everyone each day.
The way you work or play
under that sun, affects different people in different ways.
On a forage trip,
one leads, others follow!

FALLING LEAVES

Fall breezes shake gently multicolored trees
causing dry, tender branches
to cast off their coat of leaves.
Ever so gently cascades down, leaf twirling, swirling,
looping, diving, dancing,
coming to a arrest on the forest floor.
Forest's floor is covered so a winter's snow thick and wet will nourish
forest when spring brings thaw.
Circle of Life like a wheel turns around.
A branch sprouts new leaves so growth is assured when spring arrives.
Fall lets trees shake leaves off once again,
cascading down until touching the ground.

GOLDEN FLOWERS

Lure of money has often been told why
men of knowledge searched for
golden dust. This substance of glitter sparkled, beckoning man *to take a chance.*
Destiny says when traveling *Golden Road*, beware of thorny brambles
hidden inside of many pretty golden flowers growing alongside!
Things that beckon from afar are trying to
enhance their lesser hidden stars.
Destroying nature's beauty to erect manmade stone
or concrete places for humanity's pleasure and grace
only shows the stupidity of man!
Ancient times so tell of many different civilizations
that have grown and fell,
only to rise up again in another place and with a new name
starting life all over again.
A field of golden flowers call to run barefoot
through among them all.
In doing so, nature has sown beneath flowery yellow crowns
spikes of thorns, thistles to puncture and inflict *pain!*
If you so desire to travel this *Golden Road,*
stay prepared to suffer anguish when greed supersedes *refrain!*

COMMUNITY GARDEN

A community garden is a place where fellowship,
laughter with community pride,
together with love, does there abide.
Thought of teaching a child to grow things
to sustain life may perhaps one
day help that person to know.
In life, when two foes meet,
a common bond is having something to eat!
One with the most can share with the one that has the least.
Then conflict can be about who grows bigger and best.
Conflicts can be settled without *anger,* it seems,
when two people talk while hoeing weeds from a row of beans.
In a Community Garden, plans could be
made concerning local projects,
citizens' concerns, while thinning *spring onions* or cutting *collard greens.*
Without forums, boards, or legal tact, people can solve problems
because of *hard* work.
In a Community Garden, that will be the only reason
they have a *pain in the neck!*

HOOCHY MAMA

Name of my old truck that has been
stationary in the pasture for quite a
while, days before tell tales of lore when
islands with palmetto scrub would
hide a liquor still.

Down South a ways, stories told of the
shootout held over hunting rights
there among slash pine, palmetto scrub of all kind.
Then came the day when two hog claims
came to blows. Men fought in
thicket plumb. When it ended, ground was
level where they rolled around.

Open land where a man could hunt is no
longer here. Hunting clubs try to
protect a woods for sport, hunting deer.
This infringes on people's rights
to build subdivisions, golf courses, and the like.
People like me are left to passively write
about Hoochy Mama, my old truck!

FURRY FELINES & HIDDEN FROG POND

Furry felines gather in shade of late evening time
close to activity in water of garden's
frog pond. This secluded paradise spot can be
found near Big Oak Tree, under ever-
flowing waterfall. Residents live there: Tadpoles,
goldfish, algae eaters, snails, tiny
aquatic critters.
As you approach, a splash of water can be heard
signaling the rush of a frog to find
safety in the water. Moving rapidly throughout
the pond are tiny black objects. These
tadpoles will later become frogs and will leave this pond.
Around the pond grow luscious tropical plants
with large green leaves, a perfect place
for young kitties to relax and observe this
water show. Down at the bottom,
suspended motionless in time, are two big
goldfish enjoying cool, deep water,
and also shade.
Under some outcropping rocks, hidden from view, live algae eaters,
the pond's cleanup crew, along with snails
and tadpoles, they keep their
pond from turning green.
After a long morning of activity, little white
and gray kitty decides to take a nap.
Walking ever so slowly, kitty makes her way to
a favorite spot to take a hard-earned
nap. Finding a nice spot warmed by the sun, she lays down.
I slowly approach, then gently run my fingers
gingerly along her outstretched body.
Sudden sensation alarms sleeping cat! She raises
her head instantly, eyes wide with
amazement. Almost as fast, she gathers her four
paws under her body, bounds to a
safe distance, stops, sits and looks back with those same wide eyes.

I gently meow to her, and after a few long
seconds, I again emit another meow.
At this sound, kitty turns with ease of motion.
Kitty moves like water flowing down
rocks of a waterfall, bounds over a metal wire railing,
disappearing into a large clump of pampas grass!
Not far away is a gray tiger-striped momma cat.
After many days of talking with her
by meowing, mother cat will let me approach
her, also feed her, but I cannot touch
her.
She is trusting, with a wild instinct, while being wary and elusive.
Tiger-striped cat and her kittens reside in
nature's beautiful garden where flowers,
trees, herbs, and vegetables grow along with
birds, butterflies, fish, rodents, reptiles,
dogs, and humans.
All of this changes with the seasons controlled
by nature! Every day is a new
experience for furry felines around Garden's Hidden Frog Pond.

HORSES

Horses are true to life
for humanity in peace or strife!
Before a wagon or in war, there to carry,
pull, or use their fertile manure to grow crops needed to eat.
These animals were, at different times, the mainstay of life;
although today some run wild and free.
Shouldn't man plant food crops away from populations
to help these animals survive, is the question I ask myself each day.
Rodeos, pleasure rides, circuses are the ways
that horses today are used.
In parts of this world, used to farm fields
while in other parts, they are used for dog food.
The horse is, by far, useful in many different ways.
Alas, with humanity, a horse will stay!

MY CATS

Feeling of softness, so tender and smooth!
Your hand glides across and down its shoulder and arm,
sensation is like moving your hand through your hair.
Kitty purrs softly while pushing its head against your cheek
and padding your arm rhythmically using its front paws.
Love for pets comes natural for some,
to others, unknown!

MY GARDEN'S WATERFALL

Nestled between tall green grapefruit tree and pampas grass,
yellowish-brown coquina rocks lay surrounding a gentle flow of clear
spring water erupting from top, bubbling over and down by three
separate paths only to collect in a small
basin, then flowing over and onto
an outcropping ledge.
These jagged pieces extend causing water to roll forth and cascade
downward past the coquina face formed from tiny aquatic shelled
creatures bonded together centuries past, creating this porous rock.
Landing in a pool formed from falling waters, quickly, laughingly,
bubbling over and down the smooth mound and then into the pond.
Earth around the sides contain lush plants,
tropical flowers and Spanish
Bayonets.
Above, many different song birds fly
toward rear banana trees with stalks
of luscious fruit that grow.
The gentle sound of flowing water causes your mind
to find peace and reflection
while peering into calm, clear waters of the pool.
A love of this garden is begat to those
that stand or sit by
The Garden's Waterfall!

BO'S WAY

Life's train departs on rails endless, moving,
alive with moving energy.
Static energy compounded in dread, composed in vats of
motion-mindless matter.
Void of which collectively summons unheralded action multiplied by
unknown sum of which is compounded in mind through sight over
feeling, resulting in motion, speaking only from diversified actions,
the man, did he ride?
With labored breaths, as he ran trying to catch a slow-moving train,
twosome together on this BO's trail.
Together they travel towards a destination found at the end of rail!

BO's camp, nestled close but not far away, hidden in
grove of underbrush or in a gulley below, this camp of traveling gents
with nothing to show, only a spirit of revel
and following their dream of
constant travel.
Peace of mind, code of road: take what you need to survive,
not be heard or seen, be like breeze, blow into town, leave,
same as when you please!

GRAPHICS

Taking single rock or stone homeward to be erected in a special place,
alignment of which follows land's graphics.
Stars in heaven's void glisten with shrine
derived from nature's graphics,
seeing with a vivid clarity beautiful sights
found in the world's graphics.
Tomorrow is. Yesterday was.
Pure thought is graphic of today!

MY BUTTERFLY

I, like a thief in night, do snatch this
utterance from classic words begat,
in wonder may I dream of better things
on winged schemes to place in
awe this gentle butterfly captured.
Not by love's fearful grasp, only lifting a wing to right perfect flight,
knowing that touch of amour will someday in private fate cease to
emancipate one's self-felt lowly state.
Only to combine two to soar on soft breezes with new energy
or riding reckless zephyr's ghost.
Season's breezes carry thee along in unseen streams of wind on high
across rivers, lakes, oceans you soar to find warmth in a land afar.
Fate to me brought you in full sunlight
with foremost beauty only angels
dared see.
Wings so gentle they were delicate to touch, for insomuch as a soft
murmur should cause havoc to these.
Strength so strong, mountains moved aside,
inner contained controlled
by peace of mind allowing only one to witness and know her secret of
tranquility.

NATURE'S BEAUTY

In arranging mood of thought this day,
eyes traverse wooded trees, vines, pulp,
growing there, a green fragment stationary rose vine
entrenched among daffodils, petunias, fern so fan-ish green, entwined
through inner and outsides of lattice work fence.
Rose of type to grow heaven-bound,
flowers beautiful with scent angel divine,
allowing foreign objects neither comfort or rest,
protecting its delicate inner self with outer thorns
to prick and penetrate humanity skin
while delicate petals fall from around this bud's stamen.
Wafting in breezes, flow to rest, gently below
upon moist earth that I know.
Gently I bend down to retrieve this angel's gift,
placing upon delicate satin skin that I love very much.
Enhancing beauty with nature's beauty from naturally given source!
Could life give any more than its very best?

NATURE'S SOUP

In a large vacant Rocky Mountain Meadow, combine
2 mud slides, followed by 14 smelters (melted iron ore),
3 lightning bolts, 2 thunderstorms for liquid,
1 raging tornado to stir.
Add in erupting volcano for heat.
Add additional items for taste
1 northern ice storm to cool
Consume when ready.
This hardy soup known for Nature's Meal

ICY FIELDS OF SNOW

Winter winds blow across this land covered in snow,
snow so blue only heaven can see that beauty comes
from intense hazards, hazards that only you know.
Animals, many in different kinds of hurry, scurry,
frolic in or just hunt for another mouthful to eat
atop or below this bluish-white winter's groundcover.
Let earth's vegetation sleep and regenerate for oncoming spring!
After winter's thaw, buds, blossoms, newness does abound!
Readying for summer's fine show that will enhance and promote
Yearly time of play allowing yet another New Day!

I PLANTED A SMALL TREE TODAY

Today I planted a small citrus tree,
one that will produce for generations to come
the small orange delicious kumquat,
the fruit that is edible and very good to eat,
a plant that humans love to grow and to partake of at any feast.
The tree I planted today, small in size in the very least,
will one day grow big and tall enough to feed fowl and beast.
So you see, everyone will benefit one day
by the small citrus tree that I planted today!

MOOS THE SCHMOOZE

Peanut butter on crackers or chocolate brownies,
treats to eat by little moot-sees,
always means that fine little munchies are dee-licious
with Moo's Schmooze milk.
Sometimes brown, sometimes white,
every time soooo good to drink.
Hearty souls, I've been told,
drink their milk with no fuss at all.
Pooh-bear and Tigger drink Moo's Schmooze, too!
Milk with honey on crackers,
a snack time feast,
delivered in dreams by a pretty princess,
who controls the herd of
Moo's in the land of Schmooze!

LIFE'S TWO-PART HARMONY

Basics of life are being born, living and dying!
Amount of time that you spend in between determines your life.
As for Tiana and me, life's mysteries unfold every wakening day.
If you are attentive, interested, and aware of your surroundings,
life will feed and clothe you, as well as provide
music and entertainment through nature.
The universe is alive,
Earth a living thing!
When humanity becomes too greedy and population explodes,
nature will react.
Excess will die off, until reaching numbers that nature will be able to
feed.
Power of two, you and me, ying and yang,
yes and no, right and left, front and back.
Brain, is it one whole with two parts
or two brains separate in one body?
Good or bad
or just a spare?

HUNGRY

Daily meals of food for thought
beckons to all to come and eat!
No fat in food for the brain.
The faster you read,
the more you feed
your hungry mind
as it takes in all you see and find!

LOVE'S HARMONY

Jump up, Sweet Memories, and talk to me
of many longings between me and thee
of fleeting glances, touches of tender glee,
life I lead is trouble-free.
I walk alone this line of faith that is given to me.
This path has taken me close to the edge
where all can be taken in a silent flash.
Angels that care for me,
guide and protect so calmly,
soundlessly, forever surrounding the two,
Me and You!

MIND WAVE SURFING

With ultimate energy you run carefree headlong into a sea
with board under arm.
Paddling outside where the big ones begin,
just knowing freedom of riding the perfect wave
gives credence to a day on sea of life!
Getting through breaking waves is tuff stuff,
with strength, determination, finally arrival is made.
Every seventh wave is largest, so you begin to count
while looking outside for a big perfect wave that you alone
can masterfully ride.
Happiness of attack, skillfully riding, kicking out,
knowing you alone conquered a natural form that is never the same.
Each wave is different!
Realizing thoughts in your mind are just the same is the start
in an adventure of learning that is never-ending
when you enter a sea to attempt riding monster waves
that are contained in your mind!

HISTORY CHANGE

Preservation of historic past seems to be a must for some.
Others admit pleasure in sight.
Yet foreign aliens travel to and settle here
upon which they wish to bring their own to stay,
changing lifestyles, economics, politics, behavior, and lore,
thus history changes from times before!
My friend Susan tries very hard to interpret and read the logs
of yesterday.
Her knowledge at last will preserve the past!
From quiet, friendly, and fun,
to hustle-bustle, do things without care.
Alas, the serenity you once loved,
is no longer here!

DILLY-DALLY POLITICS

People, people, get on board the Rock-n-
Roll team for uplifting feeling of
freedom again.
Are you tired of being lost in the vote? Being unable to elect
the honest and just, because you can't compete
with the big money boss?
Did you ever think about people in charge,
why they run for, are elected
to certain priority positions, then retire with land and money,
yet no one else is privileged to acquire same?
These people are local or married to local families.
If not, then Big Money Boss delegates,
backs, and finances their election,
only to have things done his way to enhance his finances in money
laundering, smuggling, drugs, guns or what about prostitution
or, the old standby, moonshine liquor.
Or perhaps there is white-collar crimes of embezzlement,
numbers games, political graft, et cetera.
Who will break unwritten code of secrecy between
police, judges, lawyers, and politicians?
If these people are the base of corruption,
then different arms that radiate from the base of these arms
grow lesser arms and so on.
Everybody wants to get in on the action
and get their share of corruption loot!
Only you can change this,
and that is done in the ballot box, with honest,
unbiased overseers watching the ballot count.
Join in, Rock-n-Roll, Crew of Honest American Citizens!
If you are corrupt, we won't vote for you!

GYPSY WOMAN

Gypsy woman was the name given to a quarter horse,
a quarter horse mare with fire shooting
off of her hooves, not flashes of
smoke coming out of her nostrils as she ran.
With close-cut mane, bobbled tail, snorting breaths emitted as though
eruption of most frightening volcano was about to take place.
Gleam showing in her eyes as if the Gates of Hades were open, all hell
was about to break loose!
Lightening when she flew, not as a living
thing, but as a whirling dervish,
stepping from the center of a killer cyclone,
power of which no man has
seen before, contained in Gypsy Woman, quarter horse mare!

HELP ME, LORD!

Is what I say every minute of every day,
thinking of days to come when I
may live my life for Him!
Notions given by mental means are subject to change in your lifetime,
it seems.
Every place a human travels this day, control is held by religious play.
Death, Doom, Destruction predicted by these.
What God do you support that believes in the latter three?
As for me,
Life, Love, Happiness is what I believe.
So, Help Me, Lord,
is what I ask for.

HOLIDAY SPIRIT

Bounty of Holiday Time Down South, is
when old friends and relatives
gather at home. Everyone brings their specialty.
Times are not hard, but not easy either.
Friends come by with a bunch of
turnip greens, while a neighbor gives pretty
packages containing a tin of
coffee.
Grandson drops by with his young girlfriend bringing a fresh-baked
basket of delicious morsels to eat!
Animals are all snuggled up in fresh, clean hay, while brisk northerly
winds are singing in a low moan.
Singing in your head cries out unseen void,
calling asking, pleading for a clear mind, uncluttered.
Your mind is focused, fresh to accept, process,
deliver thoughts of marvelous places and things!
                    The Bounty of Christmas!

HIS SHOES

Who will fill those shoes when a good man is gone?
Stepping aside to let a younger person try
to do things for advancement
for humanity's file.
Among the fray, one winner will emerge, but who?
I say WHO will fill those shoes?
It isn't size that will determine WHO.
Length doesn't matter.
Game of politics is mind over matter.
So who will fill those shoes of a good, honest man
in politics today?

DELAYED FREEDOM

Shouts of being aware of capabilities afar
that without control, disaster will befall!
Are words spoken this eve to right a wrong that may occur.
Actions taken will instill hatred for a people
who proclaim *decency for all!*
Covert means used to tell
so thousands of civilians could then be killed,
attack by terrorists lead American citizens to say
Another war on the way?
President cries *We are at war,*
while Congress says *Not so Fast!*
Look, listen before we act,
then we know the *right way* to act,
not to kill, murder/mayhem,
but to exchange ideas,
Human to Human.

BACK THEN!

I remember when all thought that we were destined to be
hero or celebrity.
Today the shock is that most are still here,
doing the same as we did back then.
Some have progressed, others have *died!*
Travel is wrong to certain countries,
so tale is told.
I guess that I'll plant some flowers, maybe a tree,
to remember those that have died
and for all of those that are here *still alive!*

FREEDOM FLAMES!

Patriotism revels throughout the nation,
freedom rings loudly,
inside halls, found coursing on rooftops,
sailing on wings of *Democracy!*
On wings of freedom, flying with truth
hand in hand,
freedom oppressed in distant lands.
Alert with eyes clear, kind,
humane to all humanity.
Wings of freedom sail on wind's breeze,
never touched by hands of man
to corrupt, pollute,
yes, to this day!
Freedom sails on
before or until eternity!
Profound creed
of an Ex-Green Beret!

DREAMS

Night enlightens unseen paths of forgotten ground
where humanity has not ventured.
This path is overgrown from lack of use, wild daffodils grow in wheel
tracks worn deep in virgin soil.
Road taken, but not traveled, is in your mind!
Unseen path that is available is unnoticed.
Your mind is a private world, creating, overcoming, remembering!

AN EAGLE'S NEST

Putting a canoe in from a sandbar at the
mouth of Moultrie Creek, you
paddle leisurely westward toward Fort
Payton rounding many curves in
this ancient creek once used by Seminoles.
New features in the landscape do there abound,
water changing from salt to brackish, you see creatures of nature
feed and frolic through the saltiest part,
oyster beds galore lay with clams in muddy
stream's bed close to shore.
Songbirds, swallows, kites in trees and bushes alongside do abound
while across the marsh, long-legged cranes wade
to find fish and gobble them down.
Passing under a railroad trestle, you spy two otters at play
in the sun of this day.
A little farther away, just around the bend,
stands an ancient bald cypress tree alone in the marsh
standing defiant like a lone sentry.
There in the top, a nest has been built by two bald eagles
for eggs to lay,
reproduce, then fly away!
Viewing nature is a treat
for those that wish to see!

CIRCLE OF LIFE

Moon's sign talks of love, peace. People's way is to live and thrive.
God's ability is for man to survive. God's
reign as long as there is belief.
Way that you celebrate that belief is your
choice. If there is but one God,
who is to say that a way a person celebrates their joy to their God is
wrong?
Life is a continuous circle. You are born, live and die!
Way you carry through this time
determines the way memories will be reflected.
One thing is an absolute: If you are born, they you will surely die!
In this, where does happiness lie?
Money can never satisfy
marriage is but to create and for companionship.
In these things, love can be found,
but oft times, very wrongly used.
Is this the reason for the world's state today?
Maybe disaster is just a click away!

DAY'S FORTUNE

Sitting at your desk, trying to think of some
exciting topic to compose in
refrain concerning an astute period of life, one that all persons local
know about, but relate same in way it was pressed into my brain.
Perhaps my seeing this very episode of life
registered differently in this
mind rather than in yours!
Take, for instance, relevant things worldwide, maybe my perspective
comes from my actions while on the other side,
when in other's view only, seen one way.
Political realm concerned with leading country into
a certain direction uses means of many unknown ways to achieve that
goal!
Worldwide dominance is not relative today,
while monetary dominance
is! Factors of which dissolve into actions that are fed upon by crazed
media hierarchy proclaiming actions taken, embellished on for
excitement of public, to be first, *right* or *wrong*.
It doesn't matter if a life or many lives are lost or infringed upon
ruining all!
I think the wording goes: *Kill 'em all, let Allah sort 'em out!*
Through decades and times of past, same
then as now, different only in
ways and means, while all other characteristics are identical!
Fact is, making war results in death or destruction
in some way or another.
Results the same: one will win, the other
lose, or both fight to a draw.
Then looking back say *Why?*
Is it for humanity? Or perhaps economy?
Is making money desired before eating a piece of bread? Or when
money is so plentiful, there will be no one
to plant or harvest, who will
eat?

ANGEL ABOVE MY BED

There above my bed on dresser so old stands an angel
holding intensions of mine, to intercede
for things promised to me in progression of mind,
ability for offspring to succeed, ranch in future life for me, forestalling
hardship bequeathed by fellow man,
type imposed on success through a spiritual hand to have
requires returning to others to give as has been given!
To love one another, love as you would have others love you!
Fulfillment to fill every part of life's acre,
given while her on this earth!
Help taken from the Angel Above My Bed!

CORRUPTION WIND

Sail on, filling breeze, sail on!
Captured in mind of poetic time, place where corrupt abound,
this city named of religious Catholic Saint
stands fast for unrighteousness,
so let the wind blow!
For the righteous will come, gentle breezes will flow,
crime will subside, and there will be peace once more.
Political winds blow,
voices ramble about what candidates may bestow,
if and when they are elected.
Taking yards of linen to make a grand sail without strong wind,
this political boat won't go!
Honesty in politics
with weeds has been overgrown.
Money, clean or dirty, controls jobs,
so truth is pushed to rear,
Factor most political jockeys use today to win,
when caught in a lie, like a big hooked fish,
know how to spin!
Let winds blow so boat will sail
on this vast and open sea of life,
so quiet, unknown by many,
where jagged rocks of hidden truth lay
and will rise up to wreck your boat in times of gale.

ARMY OF ONE

Thoughts, actions, things that you do,
are these reason enough for life of pain?
Doing things that are correct in righteous folk's mind,
to save a free world from being overrun with terrorist-controlled
government of a different kind!
Army of One is to say,
citizens of this land do care about the freedoms they possess today,
will stand side by side to defend that right, night or day!
Standing beside a disabled person from wars past
tends to send message, for that while man is abundant,
war will last.
Army of One is about you.
How, when why will be asked over and over again
for actions you took in stalemating these things
from country down south!
You are Army of One,
know what I mean?

CHILDHOOD

When as a child, all that I knew was laughter, fun, and play
in night as well as day.
No fear was on my mind, as curious things, I would investigate,
no worry of the morrow,
for food and plenty to me was bequeathed by nature's hand.
With advancing from child to lad,
this allowed one to affirm their beings
was not what people of *society* had.
As a child, calmness and love that I knew
is what I have been searching for,
only for it,
like the elusive wren that takes flight,
so too, are *Thoughts of Childhood!*

CHRISTMAS

On a young December evening, sitting on the front porch swing.
Evening is young, full moon is on the rise, sky is clear bluish-gray
with wisps of light airy clouds drifting lazily through the sky.
Sound of a hoot owl comes to ear;
while sound after a while turns into A-Woo, A-Woo cooing of doves.
In the distance, a train's horn can be heard.
This alerts hounds, baying begins,
then lasts until after train has passed by.
Silence of night is soothing warm.
Colors are calm for night creatures.
Thoughts at Christmas time are supposed to be gentle, warm, loving!
All of these things are enhanced with the ancient smell
of burning wood smoke emanating from some distant fireplace,
flowing through the air in a cool fall breeze.
Rustling of leaves, shadows flowing across the lawn
lets the imagination become reality.
Morning returning to the original scene!

2001

Elation and celebration of the New Year 2001
is broadcast throughout a quiet night;
sounds and report of pistol, shotguns, semi-automatic weapons.
Sounds of firecrackers and such are not loud enough.
Explosive devices, weapons of death,
are used to exclaim superiority, I guess.

ANGELS IN THE STORM

An angel rides in the whirlwind that directs this storm.
Thought of an Angel riding a whirlwind in our mind
that directs the action,
action of love, unleashed power of the heart.
Reason for being, to carry on,
recuperating after near death,
being alone,
always drawing from far reaches in the rear of your mind,
a saying *there is someone for everyone!*

VOWS OF TWO

This day remains instilled in mind
when offspring recite with meaning words of commitment with their
other half together for life,
attending to only them and no one else.
For better or worse, happy or sad, until death do they part!
Meanings from deep inside of body coming out through inner soul,
feelings that all may see and feel coming from actions of two.
Forever may this day of days hold prominence
within parties joined together
in *Love!*

BEHIND AND BETWEEN

Times tend to drift as in time we age, peering
not into realm before, only
those past, finding a path to follow is learned from then.
Choosing the trail that will lead a person
to achieve what they want to
be, even to arrive at the end of the trail they have chosen to follow.
There are side paths that lead to another
trail or just a more complicated
trail that is connected to the same path leading to the same goal.
Starting becomes the way.
To start, there must be goals set for achievement,
after which mortals choose either to pursue
their goal or to take another
path in a totally different direction, putting
themselves directly between
what is desired and what is desired for them.
Self-preservation comes to the forefront, to take what is given or to
believe in yourself, stature, mind,
and to control your own destiny through study and labor.
Emerging as to what you have destined yourself towards, completing
your journey along life's mystical trail of
constant trials, only to realize
that they all end at the same place in destiny!

UNSEEN TRUTH

Unseen Truth lies beneath or beyond just out of reach, perfected by a
clinched fist or grasping hand. Modeled in clay, maiden so fair,
a perfect male with godly physique carries forth intensions instilled on
modern man, truth of which, never seen, belies thought in this mortal
man, alert, seeking ways to interject truth, often misused or just
forgotten is route taken by world today,
leading to repercussions, rising
to death, destruction and decay.
Beware! harkens articles written in light of this day.
Take from Romans, New Testament:
Dearly Beloved, Avenge not yourselves, but
rather give place unto wrath,
for it is written *Vengeance is mine; I will repay,* saith the Lord.
Whosoever therefore resisteth the power, resisteth the ordinance of
God, and they that resist shall receive to themselves damnation,
for he is the minster of God, a revenger to
execute wrath upon him that
doeth evil.
Comprehend in this saying, namely, thou shalt love thy neighbor as
thyself.
Let us walk honestly, as in the day, not
rioting and drunkenness, not in
chambering, and wantonness, not in strife and envying.
For whether we live, we live unto the Lord,
and whether we die, we die
unto the Lord.
Whether we live therefore or die, we are the Lord's.
Owe no man anything but to love one
another, for he that loveth another
fulfilled the law.
Let not then your good be evil spoken of.

TOGETHER AS ONE

Reading passes time with adventure, while
writing causes much ado of
present. Affixing signature to a document belies issues that cause
renown!
Today, tomorrow, or yet to come,
a person's name is their bond, as I have been led to believe.
This is not fodder for fools or rhetoric of
jest, only thoughts of one that
believes in accomplishment, to which is added all in full, *to believe in
one's self,* and you shall go far.
Eternal strife shall pass you by
while life's laughter through days of age
will be a constant Heavenly praise.
Together with love of days and family, all
shall be found together as one;
albeit many shall be apart in form, together in spirit, eternally strong.

TRYING

Did you ever try to speak what you mean
while others hear words coming
from your mouth, but register differently in their mind? Meaning of
which is fluent, flows easily through space between me and thee.
Simple, although it seems to me, creates
problems in receiving thought
once held for just and righteous beings.
Alignment through loving humanity,
creatures contained therein living
with and alongside man.
Humility with peace responds directly
through and into human brains,
causing one on one viability in marriage of two in humanity.
Whether from across a street or distant sea,
one may accept or not love given to thee from me!

TRADER OF TIME

Where have all the people gone?
Ones that were here, now have disappeared.
I wonder if time has at all played with my mind,
causing things to be taken away,
to be released in another place for *time's* benefit or pleasure to play.
Friends that together we grew, romped, played at times life stage,
depart and went our separate ways.
Some have died, but where have they gone?
To me, I still feel the same as before.
When I close my eyes, we are still together doing the same as then,
laughing, playing silly jokes, never thinking
of one day when you will lay
your head down, *never to return* to Life,
as we experienced it
as when being alive.
Where have all the people gone,
friends of mine?
Where have all the people gone,
when they die?

THE ACT

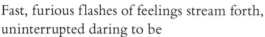

Fast, furious flashes of feelings stream forth,
uninterrupted daring to be
bold enough through tingling instance of moment gathered, rushing
through brain waves, culminating directly at crown of your head.
Feelings derived from love's pleasure coming from gentle touch or
quietly spoken words or utmost of sensual actions practiced by just a
look.
Diving into a pool of beautifully-colored eyes that have power to hold
and control actions, feelings, motions of mortal's senses.
These intense moments are fleeting; sparse
as though they may seem to
only surface momentarily and remain as long as there is a bond.
Unwritten, invisible, felt deeply enough
to penetrate the most hardened
heart, traveling deep enough into the body's
very soul, creating action of
two becoming one in action through body, mind, soul, forever in love
with each other's feelings.
Actions taken are one speaking to one, either in displeasure or pain;
trying to hold feelings back without discussion only results in violent
actions derived from commitment that isn't
total enough to hold mortal
human frames!

THE RUSTY GUN

A protest raged on a courthouse lawn,
round a makeshift stage they charged on,
fifteen hundred or more they say, had to come to burn a Flag that day.
A boy held up the folded Flag, cursed it, and called it a dirty rag.
An old man pushed through the angry crowd,
with a rusty shotgun shouldered proud.
His uniform jacket was old and tight,
he had polished each button, shiny and bright.
He crossed that stage with a soldier's grace,
until he and the boy stood face to face.
Freedom of speech, the old man said, is worth dying for.
Good men are dead so you can stand on this courthouse lawn
and talk us down from dusk to dawn,
but before any Flag gets burned today,
this Old Man is going to have his say!
My father died on a foreign shore,
in a war they said would end all war.
But Tommy and I wasn't even full grown
before we fought in a war of our own.
And Tommy died in Iwo Jima's beach,
in the shadow of a hill he couldn't quite reach
where five good men raised this Flag so high,
that the Whole Damn World Could See It Fly.
I got this bum leg that I still drag,
fighting for this same old Flag.
Now there's but one shot in this old gun,
so now it's time to decide which one,
which one of you will follow our lead
to stand and die for what you believe?
For as sure as there is a rising sun,
you'll burn in hell 'fore this Flag burns, son!
Now this riot never came to pass.
The crowd got quiet,
and that can of gas
got set aside as they walked away

to talk about what they had heard this day.
And the boy who had called it a dirty rag
handed the Old Soldier the folded Flag.
So the battle of the Flag this day was won
by a tired Old Soldier with a rusty gun
who for one last time had to show to some,
THIS FLAG MAY FADE, YET THESE COLORS DON'T RUN.

RHYTHM OF LOVE

Dancing through life's stream
as currents flow is found in everyday beat.
The step movement is played daily,
sound of which is directed in you,
which is provided by heart strings backed up by love
sung by emotions
reverberated through the entire universe stage,
to be enjoyed by an audience of one.
That is light of your life and soul,
always but a heartbeat away!

SUNDAY AFTERNOON

Late Sunday afternoon, shadows lengthen as do moods
piercing limited strength alignment through stars,
vision only says that immortality in mind may be just cries of help
emitting to their God, cast into void of endless space!
Humanity's creator is unseen
unless you look at man supposedly made in image of.
Written in forms that depict worship
you or I release spirit into sky
rising above humanity,
never leaving sight of thee
always present to ones that believe.
Four Angels guard in night or day,
Health, Kindness, Faith, Love,
of which greatest is Love,
requested by man for humanity to live a life earnestly
by including the former three!

SAYINGS OF OTHERS

Reading songs without rhyme causes me to think,
within this body of mine, there is a person who talks in thyme.
Speaking thought brought to mind,
trying to relate in this world of turning times.
Unrelated sayings repeated over again,
as if when in drug-induced mental state,
these things can relate,
only for one who is in same place could this sort of *Word Ménage* be
understood and in such belief thought to be great?
Where has all the truth gone?
Speaking words, plain that can be understood,
knowing your neighbor and likewise to you.
Life is, at times before, at others behind,
moving together in thinking brings peace of mind.
Trying times until at last, you will lay down.

SOCIAL RAPTURE

Wishing, wanting, trying to be what *social order* requires one to be,
allowing only just a few who qualify to
partake of associating with that
class of perfect people in which common bond is *what I've got*, more
expensive is better.
Being classified as *above the rest* gives meaning to life?
I find having peace of mind illuminates life's road of travel,
allowing time to see, touch, smell a flock of wild daffodils growing in
accordance with nature's call.
To notice rapture of color in your mate's
eyes when looking with serene
moments of love, fleeting though they may be,
diligent, constant, admiration allows a loving spouse this ease to
announce unseen their love beyond compare
to Husband or Wife so fair.

SPIRIT OF TRUTH

When Spirit of Truth has come, this spirit
will not speak of itself, only of
whatsoever it shall hear *that shall it speak* and show you of things to
come.
Who then today can relate to these things in such a manner as
manifested in daily life?
Knowing one's day will surely come through diligence, comradery,
enlightening of mind through studies and behavior bequeathed to
mortal man.
Stars in heaven's gate supply guidance for those with heavenly traits,
enlisting bands of angels to watch over ones born today.
Throughout their length of days on this mortal plane, every citizen on
earth has a guarding angel enlisted in the cavalry of heaven's throng
to nurture, help, and lift up their mortal assigned!

PROCESSING THOUGHTS

I wander alone in forests, hillsides, hill and dale,
searching for something.
Mind runs rampant with glee in countrywide scene
or mountain's green glen
allowing eyes to behold nature's true time.
In your life, scenes play to tune you hear, same as yesteryear.
Mortals before stood, peered, thought, were dreams ...
Same as?
In different time and space
in another's year
on same ground, on same place where feet of many trod barefoot
or shod emitting thought,
preparing ways for you to be doing same as ...
Just in a different way!
So, what have *you* done today?

SHADOWS HOOKED TO SKY

Laying in soft dry field of grass, thinking
thoughts of day's happenings
or just watching clouds roll past, thinking of each shape
and what it might be.
Birds of all different types, sailing so smoothly by,
casting fleeting drops of shadow falling from sky
to scurry along the ground and then disappear into a stand of trees
or maybe a myrtle bush
only to reappear on the other side,
to scurry more with its figure sailing this heavenly blue sky.
Everything in the sky has a twin that is earthly-bound,
traveling same, looking to be,
same on earth as above.
Where are wires, strings, and such
attaching this shadow to what is in the sky?
It is mystical how they are hooked the same, yet are free,
one in the air, the other scurrying on earth,
shadows running free!

RAMBLE ON

This is often times considered traveling, when walking down south!
Movement to carry on trusting words or poem to ramble in sequence
name of an old hound dog, speaking of a football player in a game.
Talking at length or just walking through garden park or forest woods
for pure pleasure, love of nature,
to *Ramble* down lovers lane of life
holding hands with your loving wife,
little things mean *so* much!

SAUNTERING AROUSAL OF DAY!

Tossing your head back against a soft curve
of foam pillow, you realize
morning has come and went, without so
much as saying *wake up* while
thinking of the *before* last night.
Taking slow, easy steps into bluish-gray kitchen looking for that early
wake-me-up cup of coffee, hambone buckle slowly,
drink's hot, black coffee,
while gently fingering the neck of a classic guitar
that had been left leaning against a kitchen
chair, murmuring a tune that
dashes in and out of a hazy mind through tears shed for joy
or maybe pain, trying to recall which,
so you can put rhyme or reason to a song.
Where have all the spirits gone that floated in my mind,
saying words so smooth and perfect last night,
just before I relaxed my mind?
When being in that state of heavenly grace,
one when you lay down to sleep and your
mind is free from daily strife,
someplace where you are awake *but not*
sort of in between being awake and asleep,
when all good things just come forth so easy.
Things that you say just right
and you say to yourself *I'll write that down in the morning.*
In the morning bright, you can't remember.
Your thoughts so perfect that were there last night have traveled on,
without regret you search your mind,
without a verse, your tune is gone.
Oh, but last night it was there, and I know it would be great,
if only somebody could hear.

POETRY 101

Researching of poets past noted minds
portray a piece of work is written in a period in that person's life.
Why, in righting words true to whit,
does it require life periods instead of moments of daily strife?
Decades afar will these verses written in rhyme
depict scenes past in *fear or fame*
asking that they *never* be repeated *again,*
to which they most certainly are.

POLITICAL: WHO YOU ARE!

Born in a time down south where who you are and where you lived
depicted what your status was in community.
Later, this scenario played out when leaders were chosen, or rather
people were chosen to become officers in
local militia, National Guard, or
even in high school playing sports. Team rosters were chosen by who
your parents were and their status in the
community, not by capabilities
of a person.
Has anything changed since *Cesar's* time in political society? Today,
assassinations are still carried out, families
killed, verbal hostility is used
to win political favor between candidates seeking political office.
If elected, promises made either are or are not carried out
to benefit me and you?
Verbal contract conducted by running for office between voters or
constituents, if elected, needs to be upheld.
Law of America is or is not
supposed to be *A Promise Made is a Promise Kept!*
If the latter is true, then how many corrupt
outlaws have been elected to
public office only to gain benefits for themselves, *financial parties, or
other nations?*
Elections are supposed to be part of democracy, to have a series of
checks and balances for the scales of Justice to prevail, stopping
corruption in government and allowing a *Free Society!*

LIFE'S ACTIONS

Driving thought through hail and windstorm of indifference,
emerging aghast to directions of meaning
portrayed in memory of past,
forgotten, forbidden, forlorn, only to emerge ghastly astute in thought
spoken throughout ages.
Delivering guidance to *nations* of people who follow directions of one,
only one, that has risen in ranks through deception, nay-saying and
falderal, only to receive same after reaching the top of their goal that
they have set for themselves.
Behavior through thought has confounded mental waves in humans
causing one to demand actions oft times
asking if today thoughts that I
portray while thinking of another will, in
fact, be thought of in the same
way.
Or will these pertinent active thoughts that are so relevant to me be
accepted in same fashion or understood, factually the same, as thought
by me?
Once received by significant other, you
see, do these thoughts of mind
relegate, delegate meaning so fine as to totally disarm, bewilder, pray
encircled with an insurmountable fence
called *Love* only to find all things
held in halls of mind crumble to ground in actions of deceit,
relegating one to the former of
forgotten, forbidden, forlorn, *Goodbye!*

PIERCING THROUGH TIME

Time travel is found in sleep when you dream of past days; things
persons of noted intellect indulge in daily
actions attempting to harness
this physical movement from place to place. So far, movement in one
direction is only way to travel.
Surprising as it may seem to some, you have the ability to do, to go
anyplace at any period of time. Simply relax, close your eyes, and let
fertility contained inside your mind bend
curves as you travel highways
through time, taking no more than your
earthly minutes of space deleted
from a personal life's time card for heaven!

PENALTY OF DAY

Arising to confront this morn,
confident in ways that you respond,
allowing ones that are aware to be ones of familiarity.
Days pass and this day is not the last for peace to come
and steadfastly hold these thoughts of mine
that I think so bold, without regress.
I, at times, do express ramblings of thought
that enhance man's freedom in thought
only to realize these are just that,
Mankind's Rambling of Thought
depicted before by Socrates, Homer, Plato,
all jotted down, retained for history's sake.
Could these articles be just ramblings of former three,
bored with feelings of *that* day?
As time evolves, more is found.
How will mankind describe a day in life of famous past
when things seemed ordinary, nothing more than yours or mine,
but this day written in verse thousands of days *found*
may reveal interpretation to be one of infamy
amiss from reality!

PASSING OF TWO

Falling in love seems to be a natural thing for two these days.
In retrospect, so, too, is being divorced it seems.
Feelings heighten to a pitch in some young people
that instead of knowing where they are going,
an excursion trip becomes life profound.
Stalling on tracks without any help, with goals set in mind for one,
hoping the other to follow seems lost.
What started out as an adventure into the unknown for two
has floundered amid hulks of the past,
leaving one to try and keep their head above water
so that they may live.
Passing of two, like ships in the night, is not planned for two in love.
Knowing each other without any hidden
things that will come out after
saying / *Do* solves problems before becoming one with haste.
One respecting one is a lifetime guarantee, not dismal waste.

OH, SAINT MARIE!

Beautiful woman of light, given choices to make in your days of trial,
features so pure, life sweet as honey,
flowing from cone hidden away, causing you to find celestial pleasure
when helping fellow man,
tempted not by pleasure or having more
than that which a body needs.
Caring for needy, the wounded, even lesser things than these.
Today we cry out in unheard sound
asking for help from unseen forms,
looking for answers to unseen things
having faith that justice will be done,
led by unseen hands of unseen God.

MIND'S MOOD

Faith, sanctity, spirit, faltering arrows pierce connecting links
in minds unknown, until compared with difference from,
ride wave's crest, shoot headlong down its face,
flying airborne, returning to same feelings altered in mind's mood.
Holding small, just born creature,
knowing this to be heavenly touch of reality,
why then does man's mind mood change constantly?

LIFE'S LUSCIOUS MOMENT

Able to live a life of serenity with a wife
close to each man's heart, to love
by doing, finding grace through understanding, knowing each one's
better points and not dwelling on or demeaning the other in times of
displeasure, to enjoy pleasure of the other
person and their ability to add
to, as you to them, when you face a dilemma
and cannot find the answer.
That is when your counterpart will say
Why don't you do it this way, and
everything just seems to fall into place.
Life is not a one-way street. It does have
bumps, holes, and rough spots,
with wanting to be with someone, these things ride a touch more
smoother than just doing it in your own!
Enjoying being together, doing similar
things together, whether riding a
bike, walking a trail, watching a show, or cooking a meal together,
pleasure derived from just loving to be together, pleasing her as well as
pleasing him, *no one else!* This, to me, is what life is about.

GROWTH IN LIFE

Following actions through thought, answering to none,
only to become what is in your mind saying *belay whims benefit life,*
do the right thing or do nothing at all!
Singing songs in and for life, combined with lust,
begins a new tour?
Dissembled in further news, describing ways that future fell,
smashed, broken, regenerated, put together by love,
tempered with pain, polished time and time again
through honesty, faith, spat upon or turned away
in this world I describe humanity
You or Me?

GEM OF REVELATIONS

Shaming faces with glorified veil
streaming down from clouds so white and fluffy,
fine as mist on a morning's leaf of garden clover with clean wetness,
pure as heavenly drops falling from tears of angels weeping for joy
while in heaven's holy state.
Wind flowing smooth, whispering quietly, calmly, sustaining
this mystical waft that drifts through a radiant sun–filled overture in
sound that tantalizes, tingles, and tempts tiny muscles in your face,
causing a radiant beam of smile emanating from you
and undisturbed natural God-given beauty that you contain.
Showing all mortals of power given for one to disarm hostility
with nothing more than a simple smile!
Justified by walking honestly as in day.
Not in foolishness and drunkenness
nor visiting prostitutes and envying other's possessions.
Owe no man anything
but to love one another
for loving your neighbor tells others of your doing.
Let not then your good be evil-spoken of,
as this path you travel leads you on through journeys of life!

HERALDING SOUNDS OF MUSIC

Melody of trust thrust deep into a chorus of life
as feelings tempt a sailing soul
raging sounds delivered with heart's steady beat
pound out newly found charismatic shrill forcing download into past
and rising again with a heavenly bliss.
Music created containing true emotions belonging to you.

FINDING, FOLLOWING, FINISHING

Love thing emanating from brain nerve causing body either happiness
or pain, doing absolutely *nada*, which in
Spanish means mortal's strength
faltering within a statue of bodily frame causing human's faltering
strength to fulfill tasks of living daily, creating a strong mental urge to
mate in regeneration acts for propagation
of genes likened to your kind,
meaning to establish family.
More produced, easier work should be to sustain life, thought men on
life's early road, in which you were born, marked, classified, placed in
order of *life's given position* for state of society held for you by given *race*
of people in control at that given time.
Separation for color, creed, beliefs, things of mortal man's whims,
doctrines delivered towards mortal men
who rebelled controlling their
own destiny in life.
Causing woman to repatriate feelings, and in doing so,
demanded to be recognized and as they should,
for tasks they have undertaken, massive barriers they have felled,
unseen by naked eyes through
finding, following, finishing, anything and everything
that they have started,
even finishing what man has started
but adding their way of thinking!

FLEETING MOMENTS

Coming to reality of touching, feeling, smelling today
that you dreamed about and have never had courage to grasp.
Timing each minute period in time when all you had to do was
reach out and do it!
Waiting for things to come to you or just the right time
only causes fleeting moments of opportunity to pass dashingly on,
carrying passengers of journey-wise to destinations
farther on down life's line.
Creating circus wheel to be filled through
need and dread without ever
walking barefoot through green pasture
grass, lying in world of financial
heaven believed to be owned by very rich and famous who only show
feelings learned, never showing those of their own.

GOVERNMENT CUT

Sunrise on marsh grass along intracoastal waterway gleams,
exposing nature's own early-risers, who,
like past season'ers, raise their tones in happy bliss.
Field mouse rides stem of waving sawgrass when easterly breezes puff
over vastness from shoreline to forest.
In distance can be seen outline of yacht plowing large wake off bow
heading south for fun and relaxation.
Under hammock of large oak stands a white-
tailed deer casually feeding
on acorns. Looking up, deer takes flight
into and disappears among many
ferns growing there.
As sun rises, tides change exposing shellfish,
crustaceans for friendly furry
creatures of wild using as their deli to eat. A lone house stands, vacant
now, once home to man making living from gathering oysters to sell
before Government came and cut a new waterway.
Now people live and play no this *Nature's Paradise* while killing a little
more of it each and every day!

FINDING FEELING

Nature's action is not as subtle as mortals perceive,
only consummation between two is act to reproduce in one.
Thus, a mother's love, demanding as it can
be, is but short-lived in male,
everlasting in female.
From birth to grave and beyond, finding
meaning in this thing called love,
only in childhood, as two may play,
never knowing what will happen in later days;
when all that you want to do is play ball,
shoot marbles, hunt or fish, and
other just wants to stay home, read, fix
their hair or nails, listen to songs
that artists sing.
Together as children, apart as teens,
then taken by another to reproduce.
Later in life, you again come together for needed comfort
until the end!

FORGET ME KNOTS OF TIME

Stationed on lighthouse pinnacle throughout time are these vivid
memories of life's rustic, gentle, furthermost intimate ways with you
and love of your day.
Moments gathered are not allowed to combine into eternity of further
flight through space, only these rambling thoughts do bring back such
happiness as found back then.
How is it for man to love a woman and yet
unbeknownst feelings are not
shared, crippling one so recovery cannot attempt to survive turmoil,
strife, begat through a given lonely, solitude life
knowing there could never be another as beautiful as she!
Beauty derived from within, such fair, tender, satin-feeling skin,
eyes with gentleness streaming forth, searching for a waiting soul
that is ready to embrace their steadfast glow,
taking each droplet of gleam given straight to recipient's heart,
plucking only quiet strings that belong to a personal tune of love.
Tracing time through life's most sexual periods seem truly alert
in feelings of man towards woman; this is true only because one may
relate in some way to feelings never changing.
Sexual act in reproduction for *all* things?

FINDING JOY

Searching throughout life, finding joy and happiness
is perhaps an enormous weight lifted from shoulders bent, folded,
trodden down from constantly seeking *special one.*
Apart but not far,
separate in tune, together in mood,
longing to be one!
Two cast adrift searching to be found,
alone on life's enormous sea of loneliness
in world's vacuum of turmoil and despair,
contentedly waiting consignment to and for *Love.*

CHEROKEE BLOOD

Located deep in Smoky Mountains, Hornbuckle Valley,
surrounded by growth of forest
housing nature's creatures at hand, living with man,
aloof, aware only that time has made food harder to find.
War between men who did not understand
caused blood of Nations to flow,
after which *Trail of Tears* nations did follow
allowing thought only on light, windy wisps to remain
thoughts of *tomorrow*, perhaps,
may be better days.

DEVOTION AND POWER

Of these I give to thee
flowing current continually,
devotion is held by trust, alive in love of anything given,
power is learned, built, sustained by devotion in life, love, health,
learning of anything given.
Current derived from combining twain emits realm so vast,
no mortal may penetrate with negative thought.
Always devoted to source of good, this feeling contained in devotion's
power, controlled by you for use of anything given!
Ah, life's beach, so clean, washed by waves so blue,
controlled by nature's destiny of life so true,
bequeathed from one that gives
Devotion and Power to you!

EMOTIONS

Writing will of whispering winds
through spirit flying in and out, out and in.
Arresting wings passing flawlessly among soul's energy fields.
Often times allocating enormous amounts of energy
trying to be then confronting life
to start all over again!

BRYAN'S SONG

To the woman I love that taught me to fight,
maybe not physically, but for that which is right,
sometimes I slip, I even fall down,
as the world looks at me, I feel like a clown.
As I turn to you with only a frown,
you say, *Come with me in the kitchen,*
and you sit yourself down.
You fill my belly all way 'round,
not only my stomach but my mind filled, too,
you take me back in time with you,
to walk through experiences,
the joy, laughter, heartache and pain,
you tell me these things to let me know
these feelings will all come again.
Without doubt or despair,
with only love and hope in the air.
Jesus Christ, and our family,
definitely do care.

CHARIOT OF FIRE

Writing poetry wrong creates bedlam, you see,
author of which I render such judgment no other than me!
Getting it right oft times means to rewrite words fluent to rhyme.
Doing so, meaning is hidden from view,
creating points disputed to be true!
Acting on truth can oft times be swayed
by using a word sounding better, but meaning is not the same.
At which tides of truth can be changed, placing unknown people into
history's flame, never knowing who or why?
Placing strength on wheels holding chariot's blame
to carry throughout a universe of truth
without dimming its flame!
Tiana, this is my apology to you,
asking your forgiveness, please?

ALOOF OF DAYS

Following moon in journeys across earth,
looking for a place to lay your head and rest,
constant vigilance is held for peace,
never knowing place or time when life's end you will meet.
Day's sun arises, casting shadows on ground,
showing all change of today no longer will be the same
as yesterday, causing shadows to stay ... *Aloof of Days!*
Simple love in humans instill part truth, part compassion,
part need to have a companion to pass days.
Always looking for something you seek, simple though it seems hard,
to find *Aloof of Days* to find peace of mind.
People of Nations comprise earth flow,
which carry on through moon and stars trying to be known
here on earth while eternity stays
Aloof of Days!

AGONIZING DEFEAT!

Tomorrow is another day or there is always a next time!
Often issued words of consolation to sooth a downtrodden soul,
games of yore lasted all day,
losers received death, they say.
Feelings pass over your shrouded spirit
lasting until thought is broken revealing
Agonizing thrill of Defeat!